Critical
Thinking

Solve Hard Problems Easily, Make Better Decisions, and Bulletproof Your Mind

Gabriel Dawson

Table of Content

Introduction

"I just can't figure out this problem."

"I feel like I always make the wrong decision."

"I'm drowning in all this conflicting information."

"I can't see the big picture."

"My emotions are clouding my judgment."

"I freeze up when I have to make important choices."

"I don't know how to weigh the options in front of me."

"I feel manipulated by other people's opinions."

"I struggle to tell facts from opinions."

I f you recognize yourself in these statements, you're not alone. Maybe you've faced a problem convinced you could solve it, but as you worked on it, doubts started creeping in. The solutions you come up with never seem good enough, and you find yourself wishing for a clearer mind, confused by the whole situation. Your confidence in your abilities starts to waver, and you even feel frustrated. You get to the point of wondering if it's really worth putting in so much effort.

Yet, after a while, you realize you're trapped in a cycle: you keep making decisions that lead nowhere, and you always end up with the same unresolved problems. There's a reason why you find yourself in this repetitive pattern, and there's also a solution. What you probably need is to develop and refine your critical thinking skills.

Critical thinking is simply a mental approach that allows you to analyze information objectively, evaluate the evidence in front of you, and arrive at logical conclusions. I know you'd love to be able to make effective decisions and solve complex problems, but you often find yourself struggling, overwhelmed or influenced by your personal biases. You're afraid of making mistakes or being deceived, and this can lead you to either completely paralyze or make hasty decisions.

This fear stems from the fact that many of us believe critical thinking is an innate gift, something you're born with, rather than a skill that can be learned and improved with practice. It's a belief that operates mostly at a subconscious level and manifests as frustration, anxiety, feelings of inadequacy, and a desire to avoid situations that require in-depth analysis.

If you've never developed solid critical thinking skills, you've probably often found yourself struggling in complex situations or when you had to make important decisions. This can lead you to distrust your reasoning abilities and rely too heavily on what others say or on pre-packaged solutions. Deep down, you already expect to fail or be deceived, and this triggers a defensive reaction in you: you either avoid the situation altogether or make impulsive decisions.

This skepticism about your ability to think clearly and objectively can become deeply rooted and influence your actions. It arises as a defense mechanism, born out of fear and past experiences where you felt inadequate or failed. The difficulty you experience today in dealing with problems and making decisions could be the re-emergence of these old "cognitive wounds".

This defense mechanism creates an unconscious fear within you: that of losing control of your life or making the wrong decision. The more complicated a situation becomes, the stronger your fear of feeling vulnerable or making a fool of yourself grows. As problems become more intricate and decisions more important, your anxiety of being overwhelmed, making mistakes, and not living up to expectations also increases.

Paradoxically, at this point, it seems safer to you to avoid dealing with problems altogether or to postpone decisions. It's an automatic reaction that starts from the emotional centers of your brain and completely bypasses rational thought. It works like a survival instinct: it prioritizes feeling emotionally safe over your adult desire to grow and succeed. You prefer a sort of "mental escape" rather than facing what you perceive as a risk of failure.

Your past experiences might have made you associate critical thinking with negative outcomes, giving you an instinctive need to avoid in-depth analysis to regain emotional balance.

Perhaps you recognize yourself in this scenario: you approach a problem full of hope, convinced you can solve it easily. But then, when the situation gets more complicated, something clicks inside you and you start to see the problem as insurmountable. You get doubts that don't really have any foundation, you start thinking the situation is too difficult, or you fixate on small details that become unbearable for you.

This is your "deactivation strategy" in action: a subconscious way of taking a step back to avoid feeling overwhelmed. Instead of facing these uncomfortable emotions, you prefer to distance yourself, convincing yourself that the problems are unsolvable or that the decisions are too risky.

This pattern repeats itself every time you face a new challenge, unless you recognize it and decide to face it as a personal limitation. If in some situations you don't experience these difficulties, it could simply be because they haven't reached a level of complexity sufficient to trigger your defense mechanism.

Avoiding critical thinking makes you feel less vulnerable, it's true, but it also prevents you from developing real problem-solving and decision-making skills, which are fundamental for success in life. In your effort to avoid mental discomfort, you end up missing out on the richness of life experiences and the opportunity to grow as a person and create meaningful connections with the world around you.

There are several factors that can contribute to your fear of engaging in critical thinking:

- Maybe you believe you're totally responsible for the consequences of your decisions, and this leads you to postpone or avoid making important decisions, even at the expense of your well-being. You might not realize that sometimes, instead of looking for the perfect solution, it's more important to make a reasonable decision and move forward. If you feel incapable of making the "right decision", this can make you feel incompetent and powerless, especially if you've been taught that security and personal value come from always being right. This can result in a deep-seated fear of not being good enough.

- You might have a natural aversion to ambiguous or complex situations, which pushes you to look for shortcuts or simplistic solutions when faced with problems that would require in-depth analysis. You often end up projecting your frustration onto others or onto the situation itself, seeing them as a source of irritation. Not having other ways to handle these feelings, you might have developed a strategy of escaping from your feelings of inadequacy. Maybe you seek distractions or focus on superficial goals that make you feel more competent. But when you're faced with challenges that require true critical thinking, you're forced to confront these difficult emotions.

- Perhaps you believe that dedicating time to analysis and reflection is a waste of time, and you think that acting immediately is always better than stopping to think. This can prevent you from assertively communicating your ideas because you're afraid of being seen as indecisive or inefficient.

- You might have a deep fear of being wrong, which leads you to believe you always have to be right to be accepted or respected. When someone asks you to explain or justify your decisions, you interpret it as a criticism of your inadequacy, and this fuels your fear of losing credibility while trying to meet others' expectations. The fear is amplified because you believe that staying true to your thought process will make you vulnerable to judgment, as if your authentic way of reasoning wasn't worthy of respect and acceptance.

These fears fundamentally stem from a deep and mistaken belief: that critical thinking is an innate ability and not something that can be learned, and that admitting uncertainties or doubts is a sign of weakness. The idea of having to give up the safety of preconceived opinions to explore new perspectives scares you, and will continue to do so as long as these false beliefs remain rooted in you, often at an unconscious level.

You'll continue to avoid critical thinking until you're willing to free yourself from the need to control what others think of you, trying to always appear confident and infallible. Instead, you could learn to embrace the authenticity of your thought process. This transformation happens when you stop belittling your doubts and uncertainties.

If you learn to recognize and value your reasoning process as legitimate, and if you learn to communicate it in an open and collaborative way, you'll find it easier to face complex challenges and make thoughtful decisions. This balanced approach nurtures self-confidence in facing difficult problems without sacrificing your intellectual integrity.

If you have poor critical thinking skills, probably one of your main fears is being overwhelmed by complexity. This fear stems from the difficulties you have in identifying and articulating your thought processes and reasoning. You're afraid that these processes might be suppressed or ignored, and that this might lead you to lose control over your life.

You also tend to experience an excessive sense of inadequacy that you may not be able to process in a healthy way, and this makes any situation that requires in-depth analysis uncomfortable for you. Even if you try to appear confident on the outside, you have self-esteem issues that contribute to a subconscious fear of not being up to the task when facing complex challenges, and this increases your fear of failure. This fear of not living up to expectations prevents you from developing truly critical and objective thinking.

Deep down, inside you, there's the belief that you're incapable of thinking critically and effectively. You're afraid of engaging too deeply in in-depth analysis because you fear you'll inevitably fail, and this fear is rooted in a subconscious belief in your intrinsic flaws. Your resistance to critical thinking might stem from past experiences where you felt overwhelmed by complexity when you were younger.

If someone manages to overcome these emotional barriers of yours, you might inadvertently engage in behaviors that further reinforce this negative perception of yourself. It's important for you to understand that thinking styles are not fixed personality disorders; they are instead unconscious beliefs about how to deal with problems and decisions. With commitment and understanding, you can reshape and transform these patterns.

To address these fundamental issues, you need a proactive approach:

- Challenge your false beliefs and strengthen your self-esteem: Re-evaluate the mistaken ideas that are rooted in you and actively work to cultivate a positive view of your cognitive abilities.

- Recognize and affirm your thought processes: Begin a journey to understand and express your true way of reasoning, while respecting others' thought processes.

- Learn to manage uncertainty in a healthy way: Instead of repressing your doubts, strive to understand and process them constructively.

- Cultivate and maintain a balanced approach to problem-solving: Seek, recognize, appreciate, and nurture problem-solving methods that are enriching and maintain a healthy balance between analysis and action.

- Eliminate harmful behaviors: Engage in self-reflection to identify and eliminate behaviors that hinder your well-being and your ability to think critically.

- Develop skills to resolve cognitive conflicts: Build confidence in facing and resolving challenges within your thought process, learning to trust your ability to navigate through cognitive difficulties.

This book is a comprehensive guide to self-discovery. It will provide you with valuable insights and practical strategies to overcome these challenges. Immerse yourself deeply in the content: you'll find the secrets to developing the critical thinking you desire and the decision-making skills you need to succeed in every area of your life.

Chapter 1:
The Critical Mind

"The trouble with the world is that the stupid are cocksure and the intelligent are full of doubt." - Bertrand Russell

I magine being able to navigate through the chaos of information with laser-like precision, instantly distinguishing facts from fiction. How would your life change? You would be able to make wiser decisions, solve complex problems with ease, and see the world with a clarity that few possess. This is the power of critical thinking, and you are about to unlock it.

Critical thinking is a process of rational analysis and evaluation of information. It's not just about being negative or criticizing everything you encounter. When you think critically, you carefully examine ideas, assess their validity and reliability, consider different perspectives, and draw conclusions based on evidence and logical reasoning.

This approach allows you not to take information at face value. Instead, you question the evidence supporting claims, the reliability of sources, possible alternative explanations, and any potential biases or prejudices involved. The result is the ability to make more informed decisions and solve problems more effectively.

In today's information-overloaded world, critical thinking is essential. It provides you with the tools to distinguish facts from opinions, recognize biases, and build strong arguments. It's not just an academic or professional tool but a life skill that can enhance every aspect of your existence.

Critical thinking involves several key skills. Careful observation allows you to notice details others might overlook. Analysis helps you break down complex information into more manageable parts. Interpretation enables you to understand the meaning and implications of what you observe. Reflection leads you to consider information from different angles. Evaluation allows you to judge the credibility and relevance of information. Inference helps you draw logical conclusions based on available evidence.

These skills are not innate but can be developed with practice. The more you use them, the more natural and powerful they become. Critical thinking helps you make better choices, understand yourself and others better, and navigate an increasingly complex and information-rich world.

When you apply critical thinking, you become a more discerning consumer of information. Instead of passively accepting what you read or hear, you start asking questions. You wonder: "Who produced this information and why? What evidence supports this claim? Are there alternative perspectives that haven't been considered?" This approach protects you from manipulation and misinformation.

In your personal and professional journey, critical thinking becomes a powerful ally. It helps you identify opportunities others might miss, solve problems in innovative ways, and make wiser decisions. It enables you to communicate your ideas more effectively and build more convincing arguments.

Ultimately, critical thinking is a form of intellectual empowerment. It gives you the tools to form your own opinions, challenge the status quo when necessary, and contribute meaningfully to the discussions and decisions that shape our world.

The Benefits of an Analytical Mind:

Developing an analytical mind can change every aspect of your life. In decision-making, critical thinking enables you to evaluate options carefully, predict outcomes, and make wiser choices. Rather than relying on instinct or emotions, you can base your decisions on thorough analysis.

Consider deciding whether to accept a new job. A critical thinker wouldn't just look at the salary but would also consider growth opportunities, the work environment, the impact on personal life, and other relevant factors. This approach leads to more satisfying and lasting decisions.

For problem-solving, an analytical mind helps you break down complex issues into manageable parts. You can pinpoint the root cause of a problem instead of just addressing the symptoms. This approach results in more effective and lasting solutions. For example, if you're struggling with time management, instead of simply trying to work faster, you might analyze how you spend your time, identify activities that take up too much time, and develop strategies to eliminate or optimize them.

Innovation thrives when you apply critical thinking. By challenging existing norms and exploring new perspectives, you can generate creative and groundbreaking ideas. Many significant innovations in history have come from individuals who dared to think critically and question established beliefs. Think of how Copernicus questioned the geocentric view of the universe or how Steve Jobs reinvented the concept of the cellphone. Critical thinking helps you see possibilities where others see only limitations.

In personal and professional relationships, critical thinking can greatly enhance communication. It aids in understanding different viewpoints, resolving conflicts constructively, and forming persuasive arguments. You can become a more effective leader, a valuable colleague, and a more empathetic friend. When you listen critically, you don't just hear the words; you seek to understand the motivations and emotions behind them. This allows you to respond more empathetically and constructively.

In learning and personal development, critical thinking is a powerful tool. It enables you to absorb new information more quickly, connect it to existing knowledge, and apply it creatively. Instead of passively memorizing facts, you integrate them into a deeper understanding. This makes you more effective in your field and more adaptable to change.

Finally, critical thinking is essential for personal growth and self-reflection. It helps you examine your beliefs, values, and behaviors honestly and objectively. You can identify areas for improvement, challenge your limiting assumptions, and develop a deeper understanding of yourself. This process of critical self-examination is the foundation for authentic and meaningful personal growth.

In a rapidly changing world, the ability to think critically is more valuable than ever. It is the key to handling uncertainty, making wise decisions, and creating a positive impact on the world.

Obstacles to Critical Thinking

Despite its many benefits, critical thinking isn't always easy. Various obstacles can arise along the way, and recognizing these obstacles is the first step toward overcoming them.

Cognitive biases are one of the main obstacles. These are patterns of deviation from rational judgment. Confirmation bias, for example, leads you to seek out information that confirms your existing beliefs while ignoring information that contradicts them. This can result in a distorted view of reality and suboptimal decisions. Other common biases include anchoring bias, which makes you overly reliant on the first piece of information received, and the halo effect, where you judge a person or situation based on a single positive or negative trait.

Emotions can also cloud your judgment. When you are angry, scared, or overly excited, it can be difficult to think clearly and objectively. This doesn't mean that emotions are always an obstacle—they can be a valuable source of insight and motivation. The key is to learn to recognize and manage your emotions rather than letting them control you.

The social environment and media can strongly influence your thinking. The "echo chambers" of social media, where you are exposed primarily to opinions similar to your own, can reinforce existing biases. Media can manipulate information to elicit certain reactions. Peer pressure can lead you to conform to group opinions even when you know they might be wrong.

Information overload is another significant obstacle in today's world. With so much information available, it can be challenging to distinguish what is important and reliable from what is not. This can lead to "analysis paralysis," where you feel overwhelmed and unable to make decisions.

Lack of time and pressure for quick decisions can hinder critical thinking. In a world that values speed and immediate action, it can be difficult to take the necessary time for thorough analysis. However, it's important to remember that investing time in critical thinking can save you much more time and energy in the long run by helping you avoid costly mistakes and hasty decisions.

Overconfidence in your abilities can also be an obstacle. When you think you already know everything about a topic, you are less likely to seek new information or consider alternative perspectives. This can lead to decisions based on incomplete or outdated information.

Finally, lack of critical thinking skills can be an obstacle in itself. If you have never learned specific techniques for critical analysis, evaluating evidence, or constructing logical arguments, you might find it challenging to apply critical thinking in complex situations.

Recognizing these obstacles is the first step to overcoming them. Throughout this book, you will explore specific strategies for tackling each of these challenges and developing more robust and resilient critical thinking skills. With practice and awareness, you can learn to navigate these obstacles and use critical thinking more effectively in every aspect of your life.

Cultivating a Critical Mindset

Cultivating a critical mindset is an ongoing process of growth and honing your thinking skills. It doesn't happen overnight but is a continuous journey of learning and improvement. Here are some key strategies to develop and strengthen your critical mindset.

First, ask questions. Curiosity is the driving force behind critical thinking. Challenge assumptions, seek evidence, and explore alternatives. Never accept things at face value. Ask "why?" and "how?" When you encounter a new idea or information, take a moment to reflect on its implications and the evidence supporting it. This inquisitive attitude will help you dig deeper and uncover hidden truths.

Seek diverse perspectives. Deliberately expose yourself to viewpoints different from your own. Read books and articles by authors you may not agree with. Engage in discussions with people from different backgrounds. This not only broadens your understanding but also helps you identify and challenge your own biases. Remember, disagreement is not a threat but an opportunity to learn and grow.

Practice metacognition, which means thinking about your thinking. Regularly reflect on your thought process. Ask yourself why you think a certain way and how you arrived at specific conclusions. Keep a critical thinking journal where you can track your reasoning and reflections. This will help you identify patterns in your thinking and areas for improvement.

Be open to change. Open-mindedness is crucial for critical thinking. Be willing to change your opinions in light of new evidence. Remember, the goal is not to be right but to arrive at the truth. Practice intellectual humility: acknowledge that you might be wrong and that there is always more to learn.

Keep learning. Curiosity fuels critical thinking. Never stop learning. Read widely, not just in your field of interest but also in different areas. Learn new skills. Explore new hobbies. Every new knowledge or experience gives you a new perspective from which to analyze the world.

Practice analysis. Regularly exercise critical analysis. When reading an article or watching a film, don't just passively consume it. Analyze the argument, identify the evidence presented, and evaluate the logic used. With practice, this critical analysis will become a natural reflex.

Cultivate patience. Critical thinking takes time. In a world that values quick answers, take the necessary time to think things through carefully. Don't fear silence or uncertainty. Often, the deepest insights come after prolonged reflection.

Finally, remember that critical thinking is a skill that improves with practice. The more you use it, the more natural and powerful it becomes. Don't expect immediate perfection. There will be times when you fall into cognitive traps or make errors in judgment. The important thing is to learn from these mistakes and keep improving.

By integrating these practices into your daily routine, you will gradually notice significant changes in the way you think and interact with the world. You will become more adept at handling complex situations, more resistant to manipulation and misinformation, and more capable of generating innovative ideas. Critical thinking is more than just a skill; it is a way of living that leads to a deeper understanding of yourself and the world around you.

Chapter 2:
Fundamentals of Critical Thinking

"Critical thinking is the art of analyzing and evaluating thinking with a view to improving it." - Richard Paul

H ave you ever wondered why some people always seem to have the right answer, while others struggle to grasp complex situations? The difference might lie in mastering the fundamentals of critical thinking.

Observation

Careful observation is the first fundamental step in the critical thinking process. Without an accurate perception of reality, any subsequent analysis or conclusion will inevitably be flawed. The importance of observation goes beyond mere "looking": it involves a systematic and detailed examination of our surroundings.

To improve your observational skills, start by practicing mindfulness. Spend some time each day observing your environment attentively. Notice details you usually overlook: colors, shapes, sounds, smells. This exercise will help you become more aware and receptive to the information around you.

Another effective technique is taking notes. When you observe something important, write it down. This not only helps you fix the information in your memory but also forces you to articulate what you've observed in precise words, improving your ability to describe and analyze.

Practice observing from different perspectives. If you're examining an object, look at it from various angles. If you're observing a social situation, try to put yourself in the shoes of different people involved.

This multi-perspective approach will help you catch nuances you might otherwise miss.

When facing complex problems, the ability to break them down into manageable components is crucial. Start by identifying the main problem, then list all the elements contributing to that problem. Organize these elements into logical categories and look for relationships between them. This process of decomposition allows you to tackle smaller, manageable parts of the problem, making the overall task less daunting.

Remember that observation is not a passive process. You need to be actively engaged, asking yourself questions about what you see. Why are things the way they are? What could be different? What is missing? These questions will help you move from superficial observation to deeper analysis.

Finally, practice patience in observation. Often, the most important insights emerge after prolonged observation. Don't rush to conclusions. Take the time necessary to observe carefully before moving on to analysis.

With practice, you'll find that your observational and analytical skills improve significantly. You'll start noticing details you previously missed and seeing connections others might not catch. This refined ability to observe and analyze will be the foundation upon which you build all other critical thinking skills.

Interpretation and Inference

Interpretation and inference are two crucial processes in critical thinking, closely related yet distinct. Interpretation is the process of understanding and explaining the meaning of information or events. Inference, on the other hand, is the act of drawing conclusions based on evidence and reasoning.

Interpretation requires looking beyond the surface meaning and considering context, nuances, and possible implications. When interpreting information, ask yourself: "What does this really mean? What are the implications? How does it connect to other information I have?"

Inference allows you to go beyond explicit information to draw logical conclusions. It's like building a bridge between what you know and what you can reasonably deduce. A solid inference is based on concrete evidence and logical reasoning.

To draw conclusions based on evidence, follow these steps:

1. Gather all relevant information.

2. Evaluate the credibility and relevance of each piece of information.

3. Look for patterns or connections among the data.

4. Formulate hypotheses that explain these patterns.

5. Test your hypotheses against the available evidence.

6. Draw conclusions based on the hypotheses that best fit the evidence.

However, it's crucial to be aware of the dangers of jumping to hasty conclusions. This error, known as the "leap of logic," occurs when conclusions are drawn without sufficient evidence or by ignoring contradictory information.

To avoid this pitfall:

- Be patient. Resist the urge to draw immediate conclusions.

- Actively seek evidence that contradicts your hypotheses.

- Consider alternative explanations.

- Be willing to say, "I don't have enough information to draw a conclusion."

Remember that interpretation and inference are skills that improve with practice. Regularly analyze news, scientific articles, or everyday situations. Challenge yourself to look beyond the surface meaning and draw conclusions based on solid evidence.

Over time, you will develop a greater sensitivity to the nuances of interpretation and a sharper ability to make accurate inferences. These skills will enable you to confidently navigate the complexities of the modern world, making more informed decisions and gaining a deeper understanding of the situations you encounter.

Evaluation and Explanation

Critical evaluation of information is an essential skill in the information age. With the flood of data we receive daily, the ability to distinguish reliable information from misleading content is more important than ever.

When you critically evaluate information, you don't just take it at face value. Instead, you carefully examine the source, content, and context. You ask yourself: "Is this information accurate? Is it complete? Is it relevant to the issue at hand?"

To judge the credibility of sources, consider the following criteria:

1. Authority: Does the source have the necessary qualifications or experience to speak on the topic?

2. Objectivity: Does the source present a balanced viewpoint, or does it have a hidden agenda?

3. Currency: Is the information up-to-date, or could it be outdated?

4. Accuracy: Are the facts presented accurate and verifiable?

5. Coverage: Is the topic covered thoroughly or only superficially?

Apply these criteria to both traditional and online sources. In the case of online sources, pay particular attention to the URL, the publication date, and the presence of references or citations.

Once you have evaluated the information, it's important to be able to clearly articulate your reasoning. This skill of explanation is crucial for effectively communicating your ideas and convincing others of the validity of your conclusions.

To clearly articulate your reasoning:

- Organize your thoughts logically. Start with a clear statement of your position or conclusion.
- Present the evidence supporting your position in an orderly and coherent manner.
- Anticipate possible objections and address them directly.
- Use precise and unambiguous language.
- Provide concrete examples to illustrate your points.
- Conclude by summarizing the key points of your reasoning.

Remember, clarity is crucial. No matter how brilliant your reasoning is, if you can't communicate it effectively, it won't have the desired impact.

Practice these skills regularly. When you read an article or listen to an argument, critically evaluate the information presented. Then, try to explain your evaluation to someone else. Over time, you will become more adept at both evaluating information and communicating your reasoning.

By developing these evaluation and explanation skills, you will be better equipped to navigate the complex information landscape of the modern world. You will be able to make more informed decisions and contribute more meaningfully to discussions and debates.

Metacognition and Self-Regulation

Metacognition, often referred to as "thinking about thinking," is a fundamental aspect of critical thinking. It involves being aware of your own thought processes, actively monitoring them, and regulating them. This awareness allows you to identify and correct errors in your reasoning, thereby improving the quality of your thinking.

The process of metacognition involves three main phases:

1. Planning: Before tackling a task or problem, reflect on how you will approach it. What strategies will you use? What resources will you need?

2. Monitoring: As you work on the task, actively observe your thought process. Are you following your plan? Are your strategies working?

3. Evaluation: After completing the task, reflect on how it went. What worked well? What could you improve next time?

To enhance your metacognition, try keeping a reflection journal. After dealing with a problem or making an important decision, write down your reflections on the process. How did you reason? What assumptions did you make? What would you do differently next time?

Another effective strategy is to verbalize your thought process. While working on a problem, try explaining your reasoning out loud. This helps make your thought process explicit, allowing you to examine it more closely.

Self-regulation is closely linked to metacognition. It is the ability to control and adjust your thought processes based on metacognitive awareness. When you realize a strategy isn't working, self-regulation allows you to change your approach.

To improve your self-regulation:

- Set clear goals for your thinking.

- Regularly monitor your progress toward these goals.

- Be flexible and willing to change strategies if necessary.

- Reflect regularly on your successes and failures, aiming to learn from both.

Intellectual humility is another crucial aspect of self-regulation. It means recognizing the limits of your knowledge and being open to the possibility of being wrong. This disposition is fundamental for critical thinking, as it allows you to seriously consider alternative perspectives and learn from others.

To cultivate intellectual humility:

- Be open to feedback and constructive criticism.

- Readily admit when you don't know something or when you've made a mistake.

- Actively seek out perspectives different from your own.

- Be willing to change your mind in the face of new evidence or compelling arguments.

Remember, the goal of critical thinking is not to always be right but to constantly improve the quality of your thinking. Self-regulation and metacognition are powerful tools for achieving this goal. With practice, you will become more skilled at monitoring and correcting your thinking, leading to better decisions and a deeper understanding of the world around you.

Chapter 3:
The Art of Asking Great Questions

"Judge a man by his questions rather than by his answers." -
Voltaire

W hat if the key to unlocking new knowledge and perspectives lies in the questions you have yet to ask?

The Critical Thinker's Most Powerful Tool

Questions are the most powerful tool at a critical thinker's disposal. Knowing how to formulate effective questions is an art that can radically transform the way you learn, communicate, and solve problems. There are various types of questions, each with its specific purpose.

Open-ended questions:

These questions invite elaborate responses and promote discussion. They often start with "how," "why," or "what do you think about...". Open-ended questions are ideal when you want to explore a topic in depth or stimulate creative thinking. For example, "How can we improve energy efficiency in the city?" encourages broad and innovative responses.

Closed-ended questions:

These require specific answers, often a simple "yes" or "no." Closed-ended questions are useful for obtaining precise information or verifying facts. For instance, "Have you completed the report?" is an example of a closed-ended question. Use these questions when you need quick and definitive answers.

Probing questions:

Used to delve deeper into a subject or clarify a point, probing questions often follow an initial response and begin with phrases like "Can you tell me more about..." or "What do you mean by...". These questions are valuable for gaining additional details or ensuring you have understood correctly.

Hypothetical questions:

These stimulate creative thinking and scenario analysis by posing "What would you do if...?" scenarios. Hypothetical questions are particularly useful in strategic planning or solving complex problems.

Reflective questions:

Encouraging self-analysis and learning, reflective questions ask things like "What did I learn from this experience?" or "How could I do better next time?" These questions promote personal and professional growth.

To effectively use these types of questions, consider the context and your objective. In a brainstorming session, open-ended and hypothetical questions can stimulate creativity. In a job interview, a combination of open-ended and probing questions can help you gather detailed information about the candidate.

Examples of powerful questions in various contexts:

- In an educational context: *"How can we apply this concept to the real world?"*

- In an ethical discussion: *"What could be the long-term consequences of this decision?"*

- In market analysis: *"What emerging trends might influence the demand for our products over the next five years?"*

- In a feedback session: *"Which specific aspects of my work do you think could be improved?"*

Remember, the art of asking questions is not just about posing them, but also about the timing and manner in which you ask them. A well-placed question at the right moment can open new perspectives, stimulate critical reflection, and lead to surprising insights.

The 5W and 1H Technique

The 5W and 1H technique is a powerful and versatile method for gathering comprehensive information on any topic or situation. This technique is based on six fundamental questions: Who, What, When, Where, Why, and How. By systematically using these questions, you can ensure that you cover all essential aspects of a topic.

Let's examine each question:

Who: Identifies the people involved or affected.

- "Who made this decision?"
- "Who will benefit from this change?"

What: Clarifies the event, action, or issue in question.

- "What exactly happened?"
- "What are we trying to achieve?"

When: Establishes the temporal context.

- "When did this problem start?"
- "When do we need to implement this solution?"

Where: Determines the location or spatial context.

- "Where did the incident occur?"
- "Where will this policy have the greatest impact?"

Why: Explores the reasons, motivations, or causes.

- "Why did we choose this approach?"
- "Why does this problem persist?"

How: Investigates the methods, processes, or procedures.

- "How can we improve efficiency?"
- "How was this strategy implemented?"

Applying this technique in different situations can lead to a deeper and more complete understanding. For example, in analyzing a historical event:

- **Who** were the key figures involved?
- **What** exactly happened?
- **When** did the event take place?
- **Where** did it occur?
- **Why** did it happen?
- **How** did it unfold?

In a business context, to analyze a new project:

- **Who** will be responsible for each aspect of the project?
- **What** are we trying to achieve with this project?
- **When** will the project start and end?
- **Where** will the project be implemented?
- **Why** is this project important for the company?
- **How** will we measure the project's success?

This technique can lead to a deeper understanding because it:

- Ensures comprehensive coverage: Leaves no significant information gaps.
- Stimulates critical thinking: Encourages consideration of aspects that might be overlooked.
- Facilitates information organization: Provides a clear structure for analysis.

- Promotes clarity: Helps dispel ambiguities and misunderstandings.
- Encourages exploration: Drives deeper investigation beyond superficial answers.

Remember that the order of the questions can vary depending on the context. Sometimes, starting with "Why" can be more effective to understand the motivation before diving into the details.

Practice this technique regularly by applying it to everyday situations, news articles, or work-related problems. Over time, it will become a natural reflex, significantly enhancing your ability to gather and analyze information thoroughly and effectively.

Socratic Questions

The Socratic method, named after the Greek philosopher Socrates, is a powerful approach to critical thinking based on the art of asking probing questions. This method does not aim to provide answers but rather to stimulate deep thinking, challenge assumptions, and uncover new insights through dialogue and inquiry.

In critical thinking, the Socratic method is particularly relevant because it:

- Encourages thorough examination of ideas
- Challenges preexisting beliefs and assumptions
- Promotes active learning and personal discovery
- Develops reasoning and argumentation skills

There are six main types of Socratic questions, each with a specific purpose:

1. Clarification Questions: Help to better understand an idea or concept. Example: *"What exactly do you mean when you say...?"*

2. Questions that Probe Assumptions: Challenge underlying premises. Example: *"Are you assuming that...? Why do you make that assumption?"*

3. Questions that Probe Reasons and Evidence: Explore the logical basis of a statement. Example: *"What evidence supports this conclusion?"*

4. Questions about Perspectives and Viewpoints: Encourage consideration of alternative perspectives. Example: *"How might someone with a different background view this situation?"*

5. Questions that Probe Implications and Consequences: Explore the effects of an idea or action. Example: *"What might be the long-term consequences of this decision?"*

6. Questions about the Question: Reflect on the importance and relevance of the question itself. Example: *"Why is this question important? What might we learn by exploring it?"*

To effectively use Socratic questions in exploring complex ideas:

- Start with an open-ended question about a concept or statement.

- Listen carefully to the response and formulate follow-up questions based on what has been said.

- Continue probing deeper, gently challenging assumptions and asking for clarification.

- Encourage the other person to reflect on their answers and consider alternative perspectives.

- Use questions that explore implications and consequences to broaden the discussion.

Example of a Socratic dialogue on an ethical issue:

"Do you think privacy is a fundamental right?"

"Yes, I believe so."

"What exactly do you mean by privacy in this context?"

"Well, the right to keep one's personal information confidential."

"Are there situations where this right might be limited for the common good?"

"Perhaps in cases of national security..."

"Interesting. How might we determine the right balance between individual privacy and collective security?"

This example shows how Socratic questions can lead to a deeper and more nuanced discussion, challenging initial assumptions and exploring the complexities of the topic.

By regularly practicing the Socratic method, you will develop the ability to think more critically and deeply, examine ideas from multiple angles, and arrive at a richer and more nuanced understanding of complex concepts.

Active Listening in Inquiry

Active listening is a crucial element in the process of inquiry and critical thinking. It's not just about hearing the words of the speaker, but fully engaging in understanding the message, including the emotional subtexts and non-verbal nuances. Active listening is essential because it:

- Improves the quality of information gathered
- Builds trust and rapport with the speaker
- Helps capture important nuances and details
- Facilitates the formulation of relevant follow-up questions

To enhance your active listening skills, consider these techniques:

- Total Concentration: Eliminate distractions and focus all your attention on the speaker.
- Open Body Language: Maintain eye contact, nod when appropriate, and use facial expressions that show interest.
- Paraphrasing: Restate what you've heard in your own words to check your understanding. "If I understand correctly, you are saying that..."
- Mirroring: Reflect the speaker's tone and energy to create rapport.
- Use of Brief Encouragements: Use phrases like "I see," "Go on," to show you are following along.
- Taking Notes: If appropriate, jot down key points, but avoid losing eye contact for long periods.
- Resist the Urge to Interrupt: Let the speaker finish their thought before responding or asking questions.
- Practice Empathy: Try to understand the speaker's perspective, even if you don't agree.

To effectively integrate active listening with asking effective questions:

- Use Silence Strategically: After asking a question, give the speaker time to reflect and respond fully.
- Ask Questions Based on What You've Heard: Show you were paying attention by asking questions that directly relate to what has been said.
- Seek Clarification: If something is unclear, don't hesitate to ask for further explanation. "Could you elaborate on that point?"
- Explore Emotions: If you sense an emotional subtext, gently probe. "You seem particularly passionate about this issue. Can you tell me more?"

- Use Open-Ended Questions to Dig Deeper: After listening to a response, use open-ended questions to further explore. "How did you come to this conclusion?"
- Reflect Before Responding: Take a moment to process what you've heard before formulating your next question.
- Check Understanding: At the end of the conversation, summarize the main points to ensure you've understood correctly.

Active listening combined with effective questioning creates a powerful feedback loop. The more attentively you listen, the more pertinent and insightful your questions will be. In turn, these questions will lead to even deeper and more attentive listening.

Remember, the goal is not just to gather information but to create a genuine and profound dialogue. By regularly practicing these techniques, you will significantly improve your ability to conduct effective inquiries, understand diverse perspectives, and arrive at deeper insights.

Chapter 4:
Logic and Reasoning

"Logic is the anatomy of thought." - John Locke

H ave you ever wished you could dismantle a flawed argument with the precision of a surgeon or build an unassailable case for your ideas?

Formal logic is the foundation upon which solid reasoning is built. Just as an architect begins with the basics before erecting a skyscraper, we must start with the fundamental principles of propositional logic.

At the heart of propositional logic are propositions: statements that can be either true or false. For example, "The sky is blue" or "Paris is the capital of France" are propositions. These propositions can be combined using logical connectors such as "and," "or," "if... then," creating more complex structures.

A crucial concept to understand is the difference between validity and truth. Validity refers to the structure of the argument: whether the conclusion logically follows from the premises. Truth, on the other hand, concerns the actual content of the propositions. An argument can be valid but not true, or true but not valid.

Consider this example:

- Premise 1: All cats are mammals.

- Premise 2: Fido is a cat.

- Conclusion: Therefore, Fido is a mammal.

This argument is logically valid: if the premises are true, the conclusion must be true. However, if Fido is actually a dog, the argument would be valid but not true.

Basic logical structures include modus ponens and modus tollens. Modus ponens follows the form:

- If P, then Q.
- P is true.
- Therefore, Q is true.

For example:

- If it rains, the street is wet.
- It is raining.
- Therefore, the street is wet.

Modus tollens, on the other hand, has this structure:

- If P, then Q.
- Q is not true.
- Therefore, P is not true.

For example:

- If it is a mammal, then it is a warm-blooded animal.
- It is not a warm-blooded animal.
- Therefore, it is not a mammal.

Understanding these basic logical structures is essential for constructing and analyzing more complex arguments. They are like the building blocks with which we construct more elaborate reasoning edifices.

Formal logic provides us with a framework for thinking clearly and coherently. It allows us to quickly identify fallacies and inconsistencies in reasoning, both our own and others'. However, it is important to remember that formal logic has its limits. The real world is often more nuanced and complex than the rules of formal logic can capture. That's why, as we will see in the next sections, we must integrate these principles with other reasoning tools.

Deduction and Induction

Deductive and inductive reasoning are two fundamental approaches to logical thinking, each with its strengths and limitations. Understanding the difference between these two methods is crucial for developing effective critical thinking.

Deductive reasoning starts from general premises to arrive at a specific conclusion. If the premises are true, the conclusion must necessarily be true. It's like following a well-defined path: if you start at point A and precisely follow the directions, you will inevitably arrive at point B.

Example of deductive reasoning:

- Premise 1: All planets in the solar system orbit the Sun.

- Premise 2: Earth is a planet in the solar system.

- Conclusion: Therefore, Earth orbits the Sun.

Inductive reasoning, on the other hand, starts from specific observations to arrive at a general conclusion. These conclusions are probable but not necessarily certain. It's like observing a series of trees in a forest and drawing conclusions about the entire forest.

Example of inductive reasoning:

- Observation 1: Crow 1 is black.

- Observation 2: Crow 2 is black.

- Observation 3: Crow 3 is black.

- Conclusion: Probably, all crows are black.

Deductive reasoning offers logical certainty but is limited by its premises. If the premises are false or incomplete, the conclusion, while logically valid, may not be true or applicable in the real world.

Induction, on the other hand, allows us to expand our knowledge beyond the observed data but always involves a degree of uncertainty. It is the foundation of the scientific method, where observations lead to hypotheses that are then tested.

In everyday life, we often use a combination of deductive and inductive reasoning. For example, a doctor might use inductive reasoning to formulate a diagnostic hypothesis based on observed symptoms and then use deductive reasoning to determine the appropriate treatment based on established medical principles.

The strength of deductive reasoning lies in its logical certainty, while the strength of induction is its ability to generate new knowledge. However, both have their limits. Deduction is limited by the truth and completeness of its premises, while induction is always subject to revision in light of new evidence.

Mastering both approaches allows us to tackle complex problems from multiple angles. It helps us avoid rigid thinking and gives us the flexibility to adapt our reasoning to the specific context.

In a rapidly changing world, where information is abundant but not always reliable, the ability to alternate between deduction and induction, recognizing the strengths and limits of each approach, is an invaluable skill.

Validity and Soundness of Arguments

In constructing and evaluating arguments, two key concepts emerge: validity and soundness. While often used interchangeably in everyday language, these terms have distinct and crucial meanings in formal logic.

Validity refers to the logical structure of an argument. An argument is valid if the conclusion necessarily follows from the premises. In other words, if the premises are true, the conclusion must be true. Validity does not concern the truth of the premises or the conclusion, but only the logical relationship between them.

Soundness, on the other hand, requires both validity and truth. An argument is sound if it is valid and all its premises are true.

To illustrate:

Argument 1:

- Premise 1: All cats are immortal.

- Premise 2: Whiskers is a cat.

- Conclusion: Therefore, Whiskers is immortal.

This argument is valid (the conclusion logically follows from the premises), but it is not sound because the first premise is false.

Argument 2:

- Premise 1: All mammals are animals.

- Premise 2: All dogs are mammals.

- Conclusion: Therefore, all dogs are animals.

This argument is both valid and sound, as the structure is correct and all the premises are true.

To evaluate the validity of an argument, we can use several techniques:

- Logical Diagrams: Visually representing the structure of the argument can help identify fallacies.

- Truth Tables: Useful for arguments that use logical connectors like "and," "or," "if... then."

- Deduction Method: Assume the truth of the premises and see if the conclusion necessarily follows.

- Counterexamples: Look for scenarios where the premises could be true but the conclusion false.

Soundness requires an additional step: verifying the truth of the premises. This often requires real-world knowledge and can be more complex than evaluating validity.

The importance of true premises for soundness cannot be overstated. An argument can be impeccably valid, but if it relies on false or dubious premises, its conclusion will not be reliable.

In real life, we rarely encounter perfectly sound arguments. Often, we must work with incomplete or uncertain information. In these cases, the goal is to assess the overall strength of the argument, considering both its logical validity and the reliability of its premises.

Developing the ability to distinguish between validity and soundness, and to evaluate both, is fundamental for critical thinking. It allows us to analyze complex arguments, identify weaknesses in reasoning, and construct more robust arguments.

Analyzing Complex Arguments

The arguments we encounter in real life are rarely simple syllogisms. They are often complex structures with multiple premises, intermediate inferences, and interconnected conclusions. Being able to analyze these complex arguments is a crucial skill for effective critical thinking.

The first step in analyzing a complex argument is decomposition. Start by identifying the main conclusion: what is the central point the argument is trying to prove? Then, work backward to identify the premises and sub-conclusions that support this main conclusion.

A useful technique is to create a tree diagram of the argument. Place the main conclusion at the top, then draw lines downward to connect the premises and sub-conclusions that support it. This visual approach can reveal the logical structure of the argument and help you identify any weak links in the reasoning.

A critical aspect of analyzing arguments is identifying hidden assumptions. These are unstated assumptions that the argument takes for granted. To uncover them, ask yourself: "What must be true for this logical step to make sense?"

For example, consider the argument: "We need to increase the education budget because a more educated population leads to a more prosperous society." This argument assumes that:

- Increasing the budget will actually result in better education.
- The relationship between education and prosperity is causal and not merely correlational.
- There are no other more important or urgent areas that require funding.

Identifying these assumptions allows us to critically evaluate the strength of the argument.

Once the argument is decomposed and the assumptions identified, the next step is to evaluate the strength of each component. Consider:

- The truth and relevance of each premise
- The validity of each logical step
- The reliability of the identified assumptions
- The strength of the connection between the sub-conclusions and the main conclusion

Remember that an argument is only as strong as its weakest link. A single invalid logical step or a false premise can undermine the entire argument.

Finally, consider the argument in its broader context. What counterarguments could be raised? Are there alternative perspectives that the argument does not consider?

Analyzing complex arguments is a skill that improves with practice. Start with relatively simple arguments and gradually tackle more complex structures. Over time, you will develop an "instinct" for quickly spotting weaknesses and hidden assumptions.

Mastering this skill will allow you not only to critically evaluate others' arguments but also to construct more robust and persuasive arguments yourself. It will equip you with the tools to navigate the complexities of public discourse, make more informed decisions, and contribute more meaningfully to discussions on important issues.

Chapter 5:
Logical Fallacies and Thinking Traps

"It is easier to fool people than to convince them they have been fooled." - Mark Twain

H ow many times have you fallen into a logical trap without even realizing it? In this chapter, we will learn how to identify and expose the most common pitfalls in reasoning.

Formal Fallacies

Formal fallacies are errors in reasoning that arise from the logical structure of an argument, regardless of its content. These fallacies are problematic because they can lead to incorrect conclusions even when the premises are true. Recognizing them is essential to avoid being misled or unintentionally misleading others.

A common example of a formal fallacy is **affirming the consequent**. It has the following structure:

- If A, then B.
- B is true.
- Therefore, A is true.

This might seem logical, but it isn't. Here's a concrete example:

- If it rains, the street is wet.
- The street is wet.
- Therefore, it is raining.

Can you see the error? The street could be wet for many other reasons, such as a leaking water truck or someone washing the street.

Another common formal fallacy is **denying the antecedent**:

- If A, then B.
- A is not true.
- Therefore, B is not true.

For example:

- If you are a cat, you are a mammal.
- You are not a cat.
- Therefore, you are not a mammal.

Clearly, this reasoning doesn't hold. There are many mammals besides cats!

To identify these fallacies, pay attention to the logical structure of the argument. Ask yourself: does the conclusion necessarily follow from the premises? Are there other possible scenarios that the premises do not exclude?

An effective strategy to avoid these fallacies is to visually represent the structure of the argument. Draw diagrams or use logical symbols to clarify the relationships between the premises and the conclusion. This can make errors in reasoning more apparent.

Additionally, practice the "what if" technique. When faced with an argument, ask yourself: "What if I slightly change one of the premises? Does the conclusion still hold?" If the answer is no, you might be dealing with a formal fallacy.

Formal fallacies can be particularly insidious because their structure may seem logical at first glance. But with practice and attention, you will learn to spot them and build stronger arguments.

Informal Fallacies

Informal fallacies are errors in reasoning that arise not from the logical structure of an argument but from its content or context. They are particularly prevalent because they often appeal to our emotions or biases, making them convincing despite their lack of logic. Below are some common types of informal fallacies and how to recognize them:

Ad hominem:

This is a fallacy where one attacks the person instead of addressing the argument. You might hear someone say, "You shouldn't trust John's opinion on economic policy. Have you seen how he manages his personal finances?" This argument does not address the merit of John's ideas but instead seeks to discredit him personally.

Appeal to authority:

This fallacy occurs when someone accepts a claim solely because it comes from an authoritative source, even if that authority may not be relevant to the field in question. For example: "Famous actor X says this weight loss product works, so it must be true." The actor may be an authority in acting but not necessarily in nutrition or health.

False dilemma:

This fallacy presents a situation as if there are only two options when, in reality, there are more. "You're either with us or against us" is a classic example. Reality is often more nuanced and complex.

These fallacies are widespread because they exploit deeply rooted psychological tendencies. The ad hominem fallacy takes advantage of our tendency to judge the messenger instead of the message. The appeal to authority leverages our respect for authoritative figures. The false dilemma simplifies complex situations, offering an illusion of clarity.

In public debate, these fallacies can have a significant impact. They can distort public perception of important issues, polarize opinions, and hinder constructive debate. For example, a politician might use a false dilemma to present a controversial policy as the only alternative to a catastrophe, thereby limiting discussion on alternative approaches.

To defend yourself against these fallacies, develop the habit of asking:

- Does this argument address the merits of the issue or attack the person?

- Is the authority cited genuinely relevant to this specific topic?

- Are there really only the options presented, or might there be other alternatives?

Recognizing these fallacies does not necessarily mean the conclusion is false. It only means that the argument used to support it is weak. Your task is to identify these errors in reasoning and demand stronger evidence and arguments.

By honing your ability to spot these informal fallacies, you can navigate discussions more effectively, make more informed decisions, and contribute to more meaningful and constructive debates.

Relevance Fallacies

Relevance fallacies are particularly insidious because they introduce information or arguments that seem pertinent but actually aren't. These fallacies can easily derail a discussion, steering it away from the central point.

False analogy:

This fallacy occurs when two situations are compared that appear similar on the surface but differ in crucial ways. For example: "Running a country is like running a family. If a family needs to cut expenses during tough times, a government should do the same." This analogy ignores the significant differences between the economy of a family and that of a nation.

Straw man:

This common relevance fallacy happens when an opponent's argument is distorted or oversimplified to make it easier to attack. Imagine someone saying, "Gun control advocates want to confiscate all guns and leave citizens defenseless." This is a caricature that does not accurately represent the actual position of most gun control supporters.

Red herring:

This technique introduces an irrelevant topic to distract from the main point. In a debate about raising taxes, someone might say, "How can we talk about taxes when there is a crime crisis on our streets?" While this comment may address a real problem, it is not pertinent to the discussion about taxes.

To keep the discussion focused and relevant, you can use several techniques:

- Clearly identify the central point of the discussion at the beginning and regularly return to it.

- When a new topic is introduced, ask yourself: "How does this relate to the main point we are discussing?"

- If you notice a deviation, gently but firmly steer the conversation back to the original topic. You might say: "I understand this is an important point, but how does it specifically relate to the issue we are discussing?"

- Practice active listening. Often, people introduce irrelevant topics because they don't feel heard. By ensuring you understand and acknowledge the other person's valid points, you can reduce the likelihood of the discussion straying.

- Use the "so what?" technique. When a new point is introduced, ask yourself: "So what? How does this affect the conclusion we are trying to reach?"

The goal is not to win a debate but to reach a deeper and more accurate understanding of the topic at hand. By keeping the conversation focused and relevant, you increase the chances of achieving this goal.

Strategies to Avoid Fallacies

Now that you are familiar with various types of fallacies, it is essential to develop a systematic approach to analyze arguments and avoid falling into these logical traps. Here is a five-step method you can use:

1. Identify the conclusion: What is the main point the argument is trying to prove?

2. Identify the premises: What are the statements or evidence used to support the conclusion?

3. Evaluate the logical structure: Does the conclusion logically follow from the premises?

4. Examine relevance: Are all the premises and arguments truly relevant to the conclusion?

5. Look for hidden assumptions: Are there any unstated assumptions the argument takes for granted?

To practice these skills, try the following exercise: Read an editorial or opinion piece on a controversial topic. As you read, note:

- The author's main conclusion

- The main premises or evidence offered

- Any fallacies you notice

Then, answer these questions:

- Is the argument logically valid?

- Are all the premises relevant and true?

- Are there hidden assumptions the author does not address?

- How could you reformulate the argument to make it stronger?

Remember, the goal is not only to identify fallacies in others' arguments but also to improve your reasoning. Apply the same rigor to your arguments. Before presenting an idea or opinion, step back and analyze it critically:

- Are your premises solid and relevant?

- Does your conclusion logically follow from the premises?

- Are you making any unjustified assumptions?

- Are there perspectives or counterarguments you have not considered?

This self-analysis process may seem challenging initially, but it will become more natural with practice. It will help you build stronger arguments and make you more open to new ideas and perspectives.

Recognizing a fallacy in an argument does not necessarily mean the conclusion is false. It only means that the presented argument is insufficient to support that conclusion. Use this awareness not as a weapon to "win" discussions but as a tool to promote more constructive dialogue and deeper understanding.

By developing these skills, you will become a more critical thinker and a more effective communicator. You will be better equipped to navigate the complex informational landscape of the modern world, make more informed decisions, and contribute more meaningfully to important societal discussions.

Chapter 6:
Outsmart Your Own Biases

"The first principle is that you must not fool yourself – and you are the easiest person to fool." - Richard Feynman

Have you ever made a decision that seemed perfectly logical at the time, but in hindsight, you wondered, "What was I thinking?" This might have been due to a cognitive bias at work.

In this chapter, you will explore the most common cognitive biases that influence your daily thinking. You will learn to recognize them, understand their impact on your decisions, and most importantly, discover practical strategies to overcome them. By the end of this chapter, you will be equipped with the tools needed to think more clearly and make more informed decisions.

Confirmation Bias

Confirmation bias is one of the most pervasive cognitive biases affecting your daily decision-making process. This bias manifests as the tendency to seek, interpret, and remember information in ways that confirm your preexisting beliefs or hypotheses. In practice, you tend to give more weight to information that supports your ideas and ignore or downplay information that contradicts them.

This bias is so widespread because it offers a sense of coherence and stability to your worldview. It is more comfortable to confirm what you already believe than to challenge your convictions. Additionally, the human brain is wired to seek patterns and consistency, which can lead to unconsciously ignoring information that contradicts your beliefs.

In everyday life, confirmation bias can manifest in various ways. For example, you might pay more attention to news that supports your political views while ignoring news that contradicts them. Or you might interpret a colleague's ambiguous behavior negatively if you already have an unfavorable opinion of them. This bias can influence your decisions in professional settings, personal life, and even in your interpersonal relationships.

The consequences of confirmation bias can be significant. It can lead to poorly informed decisions, interpersonal conflicts, and a distorted view of reality. In the scientific context, it can hinder progress by leading researchers to ignore evidence that contradicts their theories. In the business world, it can result in myopic strategies based on unverified assumptions.

To recognize and mitigate this bias, you can adopt several strategies:

1. Actively seek contrary information: Challenge yourself to look for evidence that contradicts your beliefs. This will help you identify potential errors in your thinking and might lead to a deeper, more nuanced understanding of a topic.

2. Practice counterfactual thinking: Ask yourself, "What would happen if my belief were wrong?" This mental exercise can help you consider alternative perspectives.

3. Collaborate with people who have different opinions: Engaging with diverse viewpoints can help you identify your biases and broaden your perspective.

4. Use the scientific method: Instead of trying to prove your hypotheses, try to disprove them. If an idea withstands repeated attempts at refutation, it is more likely to be valid.

5. Keep a decision journal: Write down the reasons for your important decisions. Reviewing them later can help you identify patterns of biased thinking.

6. Practice intellectual humility: Acknowledge that your beliefs might be wrong or incomplete. Be open to changing your mind in light of new evidence.

7. Utilize the "devil's advocate" technique: When evaluating an idea or decision, assign someone (or yourself) the role of actively challenging that position.

Overcoming confirmation bias requires conscious and ongoing effort. It's not about eliminating this bias completely—an almost impossible task—but about being aware of its existence and actively working to mitigate its effects. With practice, you'll become more adept at recognizing when confirmation bias is influencing your thinking, allowing you to make more balanced and informed decisions.

Anchoring Effect

The anchoring effect is a cognitive bias that describes the tendency to rely heavily on the first piece of information offered (the "anchor") when making decisions. This phenomenon profoundly influences your judgment, often in ways you're not aware of, and can significantly impact various aspects of your life, from financial decisions to social interactions.

Anchoring works because the human brain naturally seeks reference points when evaluating information. Once an anchor is established, subsequent assessments tend to be made in relation to that anchor, even when it is irrelevant or inaccurate. This process occurs largely at a subconscious level, making it particularly difficult to resist its effect.

In negotiation contexts, the anchoring effect can have a dramatic impact. If a seller starts with a high price for a used car, even if you know it's excessive, that number becomes an anchor that influences your perception of what constitutes a "good deal." In retail shopping, the "original" prices crossed out in sales serve as anchors, making the discount seem more advantageous than it might actually be.

But anchoring isn't limited to numbers and financial transactions. In interpersonal relationships, the first impression can serve as an anchor, influencing your future perceptions of that person. In the workplace, the first idea proposed in a brainstorming session can anchor the discussion, potentially limiting the group's creativity. Even in the judicial context, studies have shown that judges' sentences can be influenced by numerical "anchors" mentioned during the trial, even when they are clearly irrelevant.

The anchoring effect can also influence your personal expectations and goals. If you are told that the average person reads 12 books a year, you might unconsciously use this number as an anchor to set your reading goal, even if it might not be appropriate for your individual circumstances.

To reduce the influence of anchoring:

1. Consider multiple anchors: Instead of fixating on the first piece of information, actively seek other reference points. In a negotiation, for instance, research a range of prices before you start.

2. Use the "consider the opposite" technique: Before making a decision, deliberately think of scenarios that contradict the initial anchor.

3. Take your time: The anchoring effect tends to diminish over time. If possible, delay important decisions to allow the anchor's influence to wane.

4. Set your own anchors: When possible, establish the starting point in a negotiation or discussion.

5. Practice awareness: Train yourself to recognize when you're using an anchor in your decisions. Ask yourself: "Why am I considering this number/idea as a reference point?"

6. Use objective data: Whenever possible, base your decisions on objective criteria rather than arbitrary anchors.

7. Consider the context: Reflect on how the context might influence your perception of the anchor. A price that seems low in a luxury store might be high in absolute terms.

8. Practice negotiation: The more experience you have in negotiating, the better you will be at recognizing and countering anchoring tactics.

The anchoring effect is powerful and pervasive, but it is not inevitable. With practice and awareness, you can learn to recognize when an anchor is influencing your judgment and take steps to counter its effect. This will enable you to make more objective and accurate decisions in various aspects of your life, from professional negotiations to everyday consumer choices.

Availability Bias

The availability bias is the tendency to overestimate the likelihood of events that are more easily remembered or "available" in memory. This cognitive bias can significantly distort your perception of risk and influence your decisions in surprising and often counterproductive ways.

This bias occurs because the human brain tends to rely on examples that come to mind quickly when evaluating a specific situation. Dramatic, emotionally charged, or recent events are more easily remembered and therefore seem more probable or frequent than they actually are. This mental shortcut, while useful in some situations, can lead to distorted risk assessments and suboptimal decisions.

For example, after seeing news about a plane crash, you might overestimate the risk of flying, even though it is statistically one of the safest ways to travel. Similarly, you might underestimate more common but less sensational risks, such as household accidents or heart disease. This can lead to irrational behaviors, such as avoiding air travel while neglecting a healthy diet and regular exercise.

In shaping public opinion, the availability bias plays a crucial role. The media tend to give more coverage to dramatic or unusual events, making them seem more common than they really are. This can lead to distorted perceptions of social risks and influence public policies in ways not always based on objective data. For instance, intensive media coverage of terrorist acts can lead to an overestimation of the risk of terrorism compared to other public safety threats.

The availability bias can also influence your financial decisions. After a period of strong stock market growth, you might be more inclined to invest heavily in stocks, underestimating the risk of a market crash. Conversely, after a recession, you might become excessively cautious, missing potential investment opportunities.

In the professional context, this bias can affect performance evaluations. A manager might give too much weight to a recent mistake by an employee, overlooking a long period of good performance. Similarly, in project management, issues encountered in a recent project might disproportionately influence the planning of future projects.

To gain a more balanced view of reality and mitigate the effects of the availability bias:

1. Seek statistical data: Instead of relying solely on anecdotes or memorable examples, look for objective data on the actual frequency of events.

2. Consider a longer time frame: Don't focus only on recent events; consider long-term trends.

3. Diversify your information sources: Don't rely on a single news source. Seek different perspectives to get a more complete picture.

4. Practice probabilistic thinking: Train your mind to think in terms of probabilities rather than certainties.

5. Do a "premortem": Before making an important decision, imagine it has gone wrong and analyze why. This can help you identify risks you might have overlooked.

6. Use data visualization tools: Charts and diagrams can help you better understand the actual proportions of risks.

7. Reflect on your personal experiences: Remember that your direct experiences, while vivid, may not be representative of the general reality.

8. Practice emotional awareness: Recognize when your emotions are influencing your perception of risk and try to distance yourself for a more objective assessment.

Overcoming the availability bias requires a conscious effort to seek a broader, data-based perspective. However, this effort can lead to a more accurate understanding of the world around you and more informed and rational decisions in all aspects of your life.

Techniques for Mitigating Biases

"Debiasing" is the process of reducing the effects of cognitive biases on our thinking and decisions. It is a crucial aspect of critical thinking, allowing us to approach a more objective and accurate view of reality. Mitigating biases is not easy, as many of these prejudices operate at a subconscious level, but with practice and awareness, it is possible to significantly reduce their impact.

- **Awareness:** The first fundamental step to mitigating your biases is awareness. Recognize that everyone, including you, is subject to cognitive biases. This awareness makes you more open to questioning your thought processes and conclusions. Studying the various types of biases and how they manifest can help you identify them when they appear in your thinking.

- **Slow Down Decision-Making:** Many biases operate when we make quick, instinctive decisions. Take time to reflect on your choices and consider alternatives. This can be particularly useful in high-pressure or emotionally charged situations, where biases tend to be more influential.
- **Counterfactual Thinking:** Before arriving at a conclusion, strive to imagine alternative scenarios. Ask yourself, "What could make me change my mind about this?" or "What might be the consequences if my hypothesis is wrong?" This exercise can help identify blind spots in your reasoning.
- **Quantification:** Use concrete data and numbers whenever possible, instead of relying on feelings or anecdotes. Be aware that data can also be misinterpreted, so maintain a critical approach.
- **Checklists:** Use checklists for important decisions to ensure you consider all relevant factors, reducing the influence of biases like anchoring or confirmation bias. Develop specific checklists for different types of decisions you regularly make.
- **Seek Feedback:** Actively seek input from trusted individuals, especially those with different perspectives. Be open to criticism and seriously consider alternative viewpoints. This can help identify biases you might not recognize on your own.
- **Metacognition:** Reflect regularly on your thought processes. Ask yourself, "How did I arrive at this conclusion?" or "What assumptions am I making?" This self-reflection can reveal distorted thinking patterns.
- **Continuous Education:** Learn about various cognitive biases and how they operate. The more you know, the easier it will be to recognize them when they manifest. Read books, articles, and scientific studies on critical thinking and cognitive biases.

- **Probabilistic Thinking:** Develop the skill of thinking in terms of probabilities and uncertainties rather than absolutes. This approach can help avoid binary thinking and consider a broader range of possible outcomes.
- **Diverse Perspectives:** Encourage diversity in perspectives, especially in group decision-making contexts such as businesses or organizations. When people with different backgrounds, experiences, and viewpoints work together, they can identify and challenge each other's biases. Create an environment where people feel comfortable expressing dissenting opinions.

Mitigating biases is an ongoing process that requires constant attention and practice. Don't expect to completely eliminate your cognitive biases—they are an intrinsic part of human brain function. However, with awareness and effort, you can significantly reduce their impact on your thinking, leading to more informed decisions and a more accurate understanding of the world around you.

Chapter 7:
Navigating the Sea of Information

"Not everything that can be counted counts, and not everything that counts can be counted." - William Bruce Cameron

I n today's data-driven world, making sense of the vast amounts of information available can be overwhelming. Yet, mastering the skill of data analysis empowers you to uncover hidden insights and make informed decisions. Are you prepared to unlock the potential of data and turn information into actionable knowledge?

Fundamentals of Statistics

Statistics is the language of data, and mastering its fundamental concepts is essential for navigating the sea of information. Let's start with some key concepts that will help you make sense of the numbers you encounter daily.

Mean, Median, and Mode: These are three measures of central tendency that provide different perspectives on a data set.

- Mean: The sum of all values divided by the number of values. It gives a general idea but can be skewed by extreme values. For example, if in a room, nine people earn 30,000 euros annually and one person earns 1,000,000 euros, the mean income of 127,000 euros doesn't accurately represent the typical situation.

- Median: The middle value in an ordered data set. In our income example, the median would be 30,000 euros, offering a more accurate representation of the "typical" income.

- Mode: The value that appears most frequently. Using all three measures together provides a more comprehensive understanding of data distribution.

Standard Deviation: This is a measure of dispersion that indicates how spread out the data is around the mean. A high standard deviation shows great variability, while a low standard deviation suggests that data points are closely clustered around the mean.

Understanding Data Distribution: Knowing the distribution type is crucial. The normal distribution, or "bell curve," is common in many natural and social phenomena. However, not all data follow this pattern. Some data sets might be skewed or multimodal. Recognizing the distribution type helps you interpret data correctly and choose appropriate statistical analyses.

Correlation vs. Causation: A fundamental concept to grasp is the difference between correlation and causation. Correlation indicates a relationship between two variables: when one changes, the other tends to change as well. However, correlation does not imply causation. Just because two things are correlated does not mean one causes the other.

A classic example is the correlation between ice cream sales and drowning incidents. Both increase during the summer, but obviously, eating ice cream doesn't cause drownings. The underlying causal factor is the summer season, which leads to more people eating ice cream and swimming.

This distinction is crucial when analyzing data and making decisions based on it. Many reasoning fallacies stem from confusing correlation with causation.

To apply these concepts in everyday life, critically evaluate the statistics you encounter. When you read that "average X has increased by Y%," ask yourself: Is this average representative? Are there outliers skewing it? What is the underlying distribution? Most importantly, when you see a relationship between two phenomena, resist the temptation to immediately assume a causal relationship.

Practical Tips:

1. Seek context: Look for additional information to understand the full picture.

2. Question extremes: Consider whether extreme values are affecting the results.

3. Check distributions: Know whether data is normally distributed or if there are other patterns.

4. Beware of biases: Recognize when data might be presented in a way to influence your perception.

Statistics is a powerful tool, but like any tool, its effectiveness depends on how it's used. With these fundamentals, you are on your way to becoming a more critical and informed consumer of data-based information.

Interpreting Charts and Tables

Charts and tables are powerful tools for communicating complex information in a visually engaging way. However, they can also be used to manipulate the perception of data. Learning to read these visual representations critically is an essential skill in the information age.

Let's start with bar charts. These are common and seemingly straightforward, but they can be misleading. Always check the y-axis: does it start at zero? If not, differences can appear more dramatic than they actually are. Also, be wary of 3D bars, as they can distort the perception of proportions.

Line charts are excellent for showing trends over time, but they can be manipulated by changing the y-axis scale or truncating the chart.

Always ensure the y-axis starts at zero and view the entire time range represented.

Pie charts are useful for showing proportions of a whole, but they become hard to interpret with too many categories. If you see a pie chart with more than 5-6 slices, consider whether another type of chart might be more appropriate.

Choropleth maps, which use colors or shades to represent values on a geographical map, can be misleading if you don't pay attention to the choice of colors and intervals. Always check the legend and consider how the choice of intervals might affect your perception of the data.

When interpreting tables, pay attention to the order of rows and columns. Sometimes, strategic ordering can emphasize certain data while hiding others. Also, always check the units of measurement and footnotes, which often contain crucial information.

Here are some common visual data manipulation techniques to watch out for:

- Axis truncation: Making small differences appear more significant by truncating the y-axis.

- Selective time period choice: Showing only part of the data that supports a certain narrative.

- Improper use of 3D charts: Distorting proportions with three-dimensional effects.

- Non-proportional scales: Using a scale that does not accurately reflect the differences between values.

- Spurious correlations: Showing a correlation between unrelated variables by selectively choosing data.

To extract meaningful information from complex data:

1. Start with context: What is this chart or table trying to communicate? Who produced it and why?

2. Examine axes and labels carefully: Make sure you understand exactly what is being measured and in what units.

3. Look for trends and patterns: Instead of focusing on individual data points, try to see the overall picture.

4. Compare and contrast: If possible, compare the data with other sources or time periods.

5. Ask critical questions: Do the data genuinely support the suggested conclusion? Are there other possible interpretations?

6. Consider what's missing: Sometimes, what is not shown is as important as what is shown.

Remember, a well-designed chart or table should make the data clearer, not more confusing. If you struggle to understand what a visual representation is trying to communicate, it could be a sign that something is amiss.

Regularly practice decoding charts and tables you encounter in media, work reports, or other contexts. With practice, you will develop a "sixth sense" for spotting misleading representations and extracting meaningful information even from complex data sets.

Correlation vs. Causation

The distinction between correlation and causation is fundamental for critical data analysis. While correlation indicates a relationship between two variables, causation implies that one variable is directly responsible for changes in the other. This distinction is crucial because many decisions, both personal and political, are based on the assumption of causal relationships.

Correlation occurs when two variables tend to move together, either in opposite directions (negative correlation) or in the same direction (positive correlation). For example, there is a strong positive correlation between height and weight in people. However, this does not mean that being tall causes weight gain or vice versa.

Interpreting Variable Fallacies:

- Cum hoc ergo propter hoc fallacy (with this, therefore because of this): Assuming that because two things happen together, one must cause the other. For example, noticing that countries with more doctors per capita have higher mortality rates and concluding that doctors cause deaths.

- Reverse causation fallacy: Confusing cause and effect. For instance, observing that people who take vitamins tend to be healthier and concluding that vitamins cause health, when it might be that health-conscious people are more likely to take vitamins.

- Third variable fallacy: Failing to consider that a third variable might be the real cause of both correlated variables. For example, the correlation between ice cream consumption and crime rates in the summer, where the real cause of both could be higher temperatures.

- Complexity fallacy: Oversimplifying complex relationships, ignoring other relevant factors.

Methods Researchers Use to Establish Causal Relationships:

- Randomized Controlled Trials (RCTs): Considered the gold standard for establishing causality. Participants are randomly assigned to treatment and control groups, minimizing the influence of other factors.

- Longitudinal Studies: Follow the same subjects over time, allowing the observation of event sequences and changes.

- Case-Control Studies: Compare groups with and without a certain condition to identify potential risk factors.

- Mediation and Moderation Analyses: Examine how variables interact with each other in complex relationships.

- Natural Experiments: Utilize natural or policy changes to study effects on populations.

It's important to note that establishing causality often requires multiple studies and approaches. Even when a causal relationship is suspected, it is crucial to consider the strength of the evidence, biological or mechanical plausibility, and consistency with other knowledge.

When encountering claims of causality, ask yourself:

- Are there alternative explanations for this relationship?

- Does the relationship make sense from a mechanical or theoretical standpoint?

- Are there studies supporting this causal relationship? How robust are they?

- What could be the implications if this causal relationship were true? And if it were false?

Remember, science progresses not only by finding causal relationships but also by challenging and refining our understanding of these relationships. Keeping an open and critical mind is essential for navigating the complex world of data and causal inferences.

Big Data and Critical Thinking

In the modern information landscape, big data is emerging as a revolutionary force. This term refers to datasets so vast and complex that they exceed the capabilities of traditional processing tools. Imagine an ever-expanding ocean of information, fueled by every digital interaction, every connected sensor, every online transaction.

It's a phenomenon redefining how we understand and interact with the world around us.

The implications of big data reach every corner of society. In business, it's transforming marketing and market forecasting, offering near real-time insights into consumer behavior. In healthcare, big data is opening new frontiers in medical research and personalized treatments. Cities are becoming "smart," using vast data streams to optimize everything from traffic to waste management.

However, with this power come significant responsibilities and challenges. The quality and reliability of data become crucial when operating on such a large scale. Not all data is created equal, and quantity does not always translate to quality. There is a real risk of drawing incorrect conclusions from incomplete or misinterpreted data.

The ethical issues raised by big data are profound and complex. Individual privacy is at the forefront of these concerns. Every click, every purchase, every movement leaves a digital trace. These aggregated and analyzed pieces of information can reveal intimate aspects of our lives that we might prefer to keep private. There is a fine line between useful personalization and invasive surveillance, and this line is becoming increasingly blurred.

Moreover, algorithms powered by big data can unintentionally perpetuate or even amplify existing societal biases. If the data on which these algorithms are trained contain historical biases, the decisions they make risk replicating and reinforcing these biases. This raises fundamental questions of fairness and justice in the digital age.

In this context, critical thinking becomes more crucial than ever. We cannot afford to be passive consumers of information in a data-driven world. We must develop the ability to question not only the data itself but also the systems and power structures that collect and interpret it.

This means learning to critically evaluate data sources, understand the limitations of big data analyses, and always consider the broader context in which these data exist. It also means being willing to challenge data-derived conclusions, especially when they too easily confirm our preexisting beliefs.

The era of big data also demands a new kind of literacy. We must learn to read between the lines of charts and data visualizations, understand basic principles of statistical analysis, and recognize when correlations are incorrectly presented as causation.

Finally, we must remain vigilant about the ethical and social implications of using big data. This means actively participating in public debates about how data should be collected, used, and regulated. It also means making conscious choices about how and when we share our personal data.

Big data has the potential to radically transform our society in both positive and potentially problematic ways. Critical thinking will be our compass in this new territory, allowing us to navigate the tumultuous waters of the information age with wisdom and discernment. Only through careful and reflective analysis can we hope to harness the true potential of big data while maintaining our fundamental human values.

The Value of Your Opinion

For many, discovering the techniques and methods of critical thinking is a revelation. Suddenly, everything becomes clearer... The ability to analyze intricate situations, make well-thought-out decisions, and fortify your mind against daily challenges.

Before being able to see things through the lens of critical thinking, you probably felt overwhelmed and uncertain... And the reality is that there are many people who feel the same way – we are not alone, yet we feel like we are the only ones struggling to manage everything as expected.

My intent in writing this book was not only to help you navigate the challenges you face but also to make you realize that you are not alone – and you can help spread this message to others like you... Don't worry, it only takes a few minutes of your time.

By leaving a review of this book on Amazon, you will show new readers that they are part of a large community of individuals striving to improve their critical thinking... and you will point them toward a resource that can truly help them.

Simply by sharing how this book has helped you and what they will find inside, you will let them know that it is okay to be who they are and that there are others facing the same challenges.

Not only that, but you will show them exactly where they can find the help they need without having to do anything more than click a button.

Thank you so much for your support. Critical thinking is a powerful tool... Together, we can make a difference.

Scan to leave a review on
Amazon if you live in the US

Scan to leave a review on
Amazon if you live in the UK

Scan to leave a review on
Amazon if you live in Canada

Scan to leave a review on
Amazon if you live in Australia

Chapter 8:
Distinguishing Truth from Falsehood

"If all your sources agree, you probably haven't done enough research." - Lyndon B. Johnson

I n an age where anyone can publish anything online, how do you know whom or what to believe? The answer might surprise you.

Criteria for Evaluating Reliability

Today, we are surrounded by a constant stream of information. Evaluating the reliability of sources has become crucial. It is not enough to simply decide if something is true or false; we must develop a critical and attentive mindset. To do this well, we need a clear method to help us examine the information we encounter.

The first pillar of this framework is authority. When you come across a source of information, ask yourself: who is the author or organization behind this information? What are their credentials? Do they have recognized experience in the field they are discussing? Authority is not limited to academic titles or official positions. In many fields, practical experience and reputation within the relevant community are equally important.

Consider, for example, an article on mental health. If the author is a clinical psychologist with years of experience and peer-reviewed publications, this significantly enhances the authority of the source. On the other hand, if the author lacks relevant credentials or experience in the field, you should approach the information with greater caution.

The second fundamental criterion is objectivity. No source is completely free of bias, but some strive to maintain more balance and impartiality than others. Assess whether the source presents different perspectives on the topic or seems to push a particular point of view. Look for signs of conflicts of interest: does the source have something to gain by promoting a certain narrative?

Objectivity is particularly crucial when it comes to news and reporting. A journalistic article should present the facts in a balanced manner, giving space to different voices and perspectives. If you notice strongly emotional language or excessive emphasis on one side of the story, it might signal a lack of objectivity.

The third criterion is timeliness. In a rapidly changing world, information can quickly become outdated. Always check the publication date or the last update of the information you are consulting. This is especially important in fast-evolving fields like technology or medicine.

However, timeliness is not always synonymous with quality. Some information, such as fundamental principles of a discipline, can remain valid for a long time. In these cases, an older but authoritative source might be preferable to a more recent but less reliable one.

Applying these criteria requires practice and a systematic approach. Let's take an example of evaluating a website that provides information on a controversial topic like climate change. For authority, you might look for information about the organization managing the site, verify the credentials of the authors, and check if the site is cited by other reputable sources. For objectivity, you could examine whether the site presents various viewpoints on the topic or seems to push a particular agenda. You should also check for links to funding sources that might influence the perspective presented. For timeliness, check the date of the articles and verify if the information is up-to-date with the latest scientific research on the topic.

Fact-Checking and Source Verification

Fact-checking has become a crucial element in today's media landscape. It is no longer sufficient to passively accept the information presented to us; we must develop the habit of actively verifying what we read, see, or hear. This practice, once the exclusive domain of professional journalists, is now an essential skill for every informed citizen.

Here are some professional fact-checking techniques to help you get started:

1. Source Verification:

One of the most fundamental techniques is verifying the source. This means tracing the origin of a claim or statistic rather than relying on second or third-hand reports. For example, if a politician cites a statistic on unemployment, a fact-checker would seek out the original data from the national statistics office rather than relying on the politician's press release.

2. Contextualization:

Information, even if technically true, can be misleading if presented out of context. Fact-checkers strive to provide the full context, which may include historical trends, relevant comparisons, or crucial background information. For instance, a claim about a rise in crime in a city might be technically correct for a specific year but misleading if not considering the long-term trend showing an overall decline in crime.

3. Image and Video Verification:

Verifying images and videos has become particularly important in the age of social media. Fact-checkers use tools like reverse image search to verify the authenticity and origin of visual content. They can also examine image metadata to verify details such as the date and location where they were taken.

Fortunately, many of these professional tools are now available to the general public. Websites like Snopes, FactCheck.org, and PolitiFact offer detailed verifications of popular claims and controversies. Tools like Google Reverse Image Search or TinEye allow anyone to verify the authenticity of online images.

Developing a Critical Approach:

1. Ask the Right Questions: Start by asking critical questions: Who is the source of this information? What evidence is provided to support it? Are there other sources that confirm or contradict this claim?

2. Triangulate Sources: Instead of relying on a single source, seek confirmations from multiple independent sources. If several reliable and independent sources report the same information, the likelihood of its accuracy increases. However, be wary of the "echo effect," where many sources repeat the same information without independent verification.

3. Recognize Personal Biases: It's important to acknowledge personal biases when verifying information. We are naturally inclined to accept information that confirms our pre-existing beliefs and to be more skeptical of information that challenges them. An effective fact-checker must be willing to question even their most cherished beliefs.

Using Available Tools:

- Websites for Verification: Utilize websites like Snopes, FactCheck.org, and PolitiFact for detailed verifications.

- Image Verification Tools: Employ tools like Google Reverse Image Search or TinEye to check the authenticity of images.

Fact-checking requires time and effort, but it is a crucial investment in the information age. Not only does it protect you from misinformation, but it also helps you develop a deeper and more nuanced understanding of the world around you. Every time you verify a claim, you contribute to creating a healthier and more reliable information ecosystem.

Fact-checking is not just a technical skill but a mindset. It involves cultivating a healthy dose of skepticism combined with a willingness to follow the evidence wherever it leads. With practice, it will become a natural reflex, an integral part of how you interact with the world of information.

Recognizing Disinformation

In today's information landscape, distinguishing between truth and falsehood has become increasingly challenging. To navigate these murky waters effectively, it's essential to understand the different facets of disinformation. Misinformation, disinformation, and malinformation are three distinct concepts that are often confused.

Misinformation refers to the unintentional spread of false or inaccurate information. It can stem from honest mistakes, misunderstandings, or simple ignorance. A common example might be sharing a satirical article as if it were real news, without recognizing its humorous nature.

Disinformation, on the other hand, is more insidious. It involves the deliberate creation and dissemination of false or misleading information with the intent to deceive. This often has political, economic, or ideological motivations. A notable case might be an orchestrated campaign to influence public opinion on a political issue by spreading fabricated news.

Malinformation occupies a specific space in this spectrum. It involves the use of true information to cause harm, often by disclosing data that should remain private. An example could be the unauthorized release of personal information about an individual to discredit them.

To recognize disinformation, it is crucial to be aware of the common techniques used to spread it. One of the most widespread methods is the use of clickbait headlines, designed to provoke a strong emotional reaction and encourage rapid sharing, often at the expense of accuracy. These headlines can be misleading or even completely disconnected from the actual content of the article.

Another frequent technique is the creation of emotionally charged content. These pieces aim to elicit strong reactions like anger, fear, or outrage, clouding the reader's critical judgment. The goal is to make people react and share based on emotion rather than rational reflection.

With advances in technology, the manipulation of images and videos has become increasingly sophisticated. Deepfakes, manipulated videos that appear authentic, pose a particular challenge. These can depict people saying or doing things they never actually said or did, making it extremely difficult to distinguish between true and false without specialized tools.

Conspiracy theories are another pervasive form of disinformation. These narratives often rely on a mix of real facts, speculation, and outright fabrications, creating a story that seems plausible but is fundamentally misleading. Conspiracy theories can be particularly convincing because they offer simple explanations for complex problems and often appeal to a sense of belonging or privileged knowledge.

To identify and counter disinformation, it's useful to develop a set of mental habits. First, cultivate a healthy skepticism. If a piece of news seems too extraordinary or perfectly aligned with your beliefs, it might warrant closer scrutiny. Always check the original source of the information and seek confirmation from other reliable and independent sources.

Pay attention to the language used. An overly emotional or sensationalistic tone can be a red flag. Similarly, be wary of claims that appeal to "secret knowledge" or suggest that all recognized experts are wrong. These are often tactics used to bypass critical thinking and appeal directly to emotions or biases.

It's essential to be aware of your own cognitive biases. We are all more inclined to believe information that confirms our existing beliefs, a phenomenon known as confirmation bias. Strive to be critical even of news that you like or that supports your opinions. This can be difficult, but it is crucial for maintaining a balanced and accurate view of reality.

In countering disinformation, consider the most effective approach. Engaging in heated online debates rarely changes opinions and can lead to entrenched positions. Often, sharing accurate and well-documented information, accompanied by respectful dialogue, can be more effective in the long term. The goal should be to promote a healthier informational environment rather than "winning" individual arguments.

Building a Balanced Media Diet

In an era where information is omnipresent and easily accessible, the challenge is not so much finding information as it is selecting and balancing it effectively. Building a balanced media diet is essential for developing an accurate and nuanced understanding of the world around us.

The first step towards a balanced media diet is becoming aware of your own biases and preferences. Each of us has natural inclinations toward certain sources of information or types of news. These preferences are often rooted in our personal experiences, education, and values. Recognizing them is crucial because it allows us to identify potential gaps in our informational diet.

Once we identify our tendencies, the next step is to actively seek to broaden them. This does not necessarily mean giving equal weight to all opinions, especially extreme or factually unsupported ones. Rather, it involves understanding how different people interpret the same events or information. Exposing yourself to diverse viewpoints not only enriches your understanding but also helps you reinforce or reconsider your positions in a more informed manner.

A practical approach to building a balanced media diet is creating a diversified media consumption plan. This might include a mix of various sources:

- Newspapers and magazines with different political leanings: This helps to obtain a range of perspectives on controversial issues.

- International news sources: To gain a more global view of events and overcome the bias of one's national context.

- Specialized publications in your areas of interest: For in-depth coverage of specific topics that general media may not offer.

- Podcasts and radio programs: These offer deep dives into complex topics, allowing for extended exploration.

- Social media: Used cautiously and with an awareness of its limitations, it can provide real-time news and follow experts and commentators from various fields.

It is also important to vary the formats in which you consume information. Reading long, in-depth articles can provide a detailed understanding of complex issues. On the other hand, short news videos can offer quick updates on ongoing events. Listening to podcasts during commutes can be an efficient way to stay informed. This variety not only keeps your interest but also helps you understand how different media present and frame information.

A key concept to understand and counteract is that of "echo chambers." These are environments, often online, where people encounter only information and opinions that reflect and reinforce their own beliefs. Social media, with its personalized algorithms, is particularly prone to creating these echo chambers. To avoid getting trapped in these closed information spaces, a proactive approach is necessary:

- Deliberately follow sources and people you don't always agree with: This doesn't mean exposing yourself to extreme views or disinformation but rather to different but well-argued perspectives.

- Engage in respectful discussions with people who have different opinions: This can happen online but also in real-life contexts like book clubs, discussion groups, or community events.

- Regularly challenge your beliefs by actively seeking information that contradicts them: This exercise of "self-fact-checking" can be enlightening and helps you strengthen or modify your opinions on a more solid basis.

- Use tools and settings that reduce content personalization on social media: Some browsers and extensions offer options to view more diverse news feeds.

In constructing a balanced media diet, it's crucial to consider quality as well as diversity of sources. Not all information sources are created equal. Prioritize those that demonstrate a commitment to accuracy, fact-checking, and error correction. Sources that cite their references, provide context, and present multiple viewpoints on controversial issues are generally more reliable.

Finally, regularly practice "media detoxification." Information overload can lead to stress, anxiety, and a decreased ability to critically process information. Set limits on your news consumption and allow yourself periods of disconnection. This not only benefits mental well-being but can also improve your ability to process and reflect on information when you are actively engaged in media consumption.

Building and maintaining a balanced media diet is an ongoing process that requires awareness, effort, and flexibility. There is no one-size-fits-all formula, but rather a personalized approach that evolves with time and experience. The ultimate goal is not necessarily to change your opinions but to develop a richer and more nuanced understanding of the world, enhancing your ability to navigate the complex contemporary information landscape.

Chapter 9:
Creative Problem Solving

"You cannot solve a problem with the same kind of thinking that created it." - Albert Einstein

What if I told you that the solution to your most pressing problem is already in your mind, hidden behind a wall of conventional thinking?

In this chapter, we will explore the vast potential of creative problem solving, an approach that will enable you to overcome seemingly insurmountable obstacles and find innovative solutions to complex challenges. You will learn to see problems from new perspectives, generate original ideas, and implement effective solutions. Whether you are a professional facing business challenges, a student tackling demanding projects, or simply someone looking to improve your daily life, the techniques you discover here will equip you with the tools to transform obstacles into opportunities for growth and innovation.

Definition and Analysis of the Problem

The first crucial step in creative problem solving is the correct definition and analysis of the problem. Often, what we initially perceive as the problem is merely a symptom of a deeper issue. Learning to identify and clearly define the real problem is essential for finding effective and lasting solutions.

One effective technique for identifying the true problem is the "5 Whys" method. Originally developed by Sakichi Toyoda and widely used in the Toyota production system, this technique involves asking "why" at least five times in response to an apparent problem. Each answer forms the basis for the next question. For example:

Apparent problem: Our product is not selling well.

1. Why? Because customers are not buying it.

2. Why are customers not buying it? Because they are not aware of the product.

3. Why are they not aware of the product? Because our marketing strategy is not effective.

4. Why is our marketing strategy not effective? Because we do not have a good understanding of our target audience.

5. Why do we not understand our target audience well? Because we did not conduct thorough market research.

In this example, what initially seemed like a sales problem turns out to be a lack of understanding of the target market. Defining the problem in this way opens the door to more targeted and effective solutions.

Another useful technique is the "Eisenhower Matrix," which helps distinguish between urgent and important problems. This matrix divides problems into four quadrants:

- Urgent and Important: Problems to be addressed immediately.

- Important but Not Urgent: Problems to be planned and addressed strategically.

- Urgent but Not Important: Problems to be delegated if possible.

- Not Urgent and Not Important: Problems to be eliminated or minimized.

Using this matrix allows you to focus your energy on the problems that will have the greatest impact.

Considering different perspectives in defining the problem is crucial for a comprehensive understanding. Edward de Bono's "Six Thinking Hats" technique can be helpful in this context. This technique encourages examining the problem from six different angles:

- White Hat: Facts and objective information.
- Red Hat: Emotions and intuitions.
- Black Hat: Risks and potential problems.
- Yellow Hat: Opportunities and benefits.
- Green Hat: Creativity and new ideas.
- Blue Hat: Process and management of thinking.

By using this method, you can ensure that you consider the problem from all relevant angles, avoiding the oversight of important aspects.

To break down complex problems into manageable components, the "Problem Tree" technique can be very effective. This technique involves visually representing the central problem as the trunk of a tree, with the causes of the problem as roots and the effects as branches. This approach helps to visualize the interconnections between various aspects of the problem and can reveal intervention points that were not immediately obvious.

Another useful tool is the Mind Map. Starting from the central problem at the center, you can branch out in various directions, exploring different dimensions of the problem. This method is particularly useful for problems with many interconnected variables, as it allows you to visualize the relationships between different aspects of the problem.

Finally, it is important to remember that problem definition is not a static process. As you gather more information and gain new perspectives, your understanding of the problem may evolve. Being open to revisiting and redefining the problem throughout the problem-solving process is essential for arriving at truly effective solutions.

Accurate definition and deep analysis of the problem are fundamental to the success of creative problem solving. These techniques will help you go beyond superficial appearances and identify the real roots of the problems you face, laying the foundation for innovative and effective solutions.

Brainstorming Techniques

Brainstorming is a key element of creative problem-solving, enabling the generation of a wide range of ideas and potential solutions. There are various brainstorming methodologies, each with its strengths and specific applications.

One of the most well-known techniques is Mind Mapping, developed by Tony Buzan. This technique uses a visual approach to organize and generate ideas. It starts by writing the central problem or theme in the center of a page, and then branching out related ideas in all directions. Each main branch can have further sub-branches, creating a tree-like structure. Mind Mapping leverages the brain's natural tendency to think associatively, allowing for the exploration of unexpected connections between different ideas.

Another effective methodology is SCAMPER, an acronym standing for Substitute, Combine, Adapt, Modify, Put to other uses, Eliminate, and Rearrange. This technique provides a series of prompts to generate new ideas:

- Substitute: What can we substitute to improve?
- Combine: What ideas or components can we combine?
- Adapt: How can we adapt this solution from another context?
- Modify: What can we modify or magnify?

- Put to other uses: How can we use this solution differently?

- Eliminate: What can we simplify or eliminate?

- Rearrange: How can we reorganize or reverse elements?

SCAMPER is particularly useful for finding new approaches to familiar problems or for improving existing products and processes.

Edward de Bono's "Six Thinking Hats" technique, mentioned in the previous section, can also be adapted as a brainstorming method. In this context, participants "wear" each hat in turn, generating ideas from different perspectives.

To create an environment that fosters creative thinking during brainstorming sessions, consider the following factors:

- Physical Space: A bright, comfortable, and flexible environment can stimulate creativity. Using whiteboards, post-it notes, and other visual tools can help capture and organize ideas.

- Psychological Atmosphere: It's crucial to create an atmosphere where everyone feels free to express ideas without fear of judgment. The key principle is "quantity over quality" during the initial idea generation phase.

- Diversity of Participants: Including people with diverse backgrounds and perspectives can lead to a broader range of ideas and potential solutions.

- Timing: Brainstorming sessions are often more effective when time-limited, with regular breaks to maintain high energy and focus.

Here are some essential guidelines for conducting effective brainstorming sessions:

- Clearly Define the Objective: Ensure that all participants understand the problem or challenge at hand.

- Establish Ground Rules: For example, "no criticism during the idea generation phase" and "build on others' ideas."

- Encourage Wild Thinking: Ideas that seem absurd can often lead to innovative solutions.

- Use Visual Stimuli or Prompts: Images, objects, or provocative questions can stimulate new directions of thought.

- Document All Ideas: Ensure that every idea is recorded, no matter how irrelevant it may seem at the moment.

- Build on Others' Ideas: Encourage participants to develop and combine others' ideas.

- Convergence Phase: After the idea generation phase, spend time grouping, categorizing, and prioritizing the ideas generated.

An interesting variant of traditional brainstorming is "brainwriting." In this technique, participants write their ideas individually before sharing them with the group. This can be particularly useful for including the voices of more introverted participants or for avoiding groupthink.

Finally, it is important to remember that brainstorming doesn't have to be a one-time event. "Incremental brainstorming" involves shorter, more frequent sessions, allowing participants to reflect on and further develop ideas between sessions.

Mastering various brainstorming techniques and knowing how to create the right environment for idea generation are fundamental skills in creative problem-solving. These abilities will enable you to unlock the creative potential of yourself and your team, paving the way for innovative and unexpected solutions.

Evaluating Solutions

After generating a wide range of ideas through brainstorming, the next step in creative problem solving is the critical evaluation of the proposed solutions. This phase is crucial for transforming creative ideas into practical and implementable solutions.

To assess the effectiveness and feasibility of the proposed solutions, it's helpful to establish a set of objective criteria. These might include:

- Relevance: How well does the solution address the original problem?

- Feasibility: Can the solution be implemented with the available resources?

- Impact: What effect will the solution have on the problem and the surrounding environment?

- Cost: What are the financial and non-financial costs associated with implementation?

- Time: How long will implementation take, and when will results be seen?

- Risks: What are the potential risks or negative side effects?

- Acceptability: Will the solution be accepted by relevant stakeholders?

- Scalability: Can the solution be scaled up or adapted in the future if necessary?

An effective technique for applying these criteria is the decision matrix. In this matrix, the proposed solutions are listed in the rows, while the evaluation criteria are in the columns. Each solution is then evaluated against each criterion, assigning a score (e.g., from 1 to 5). By summing the scores, you can obtain an objective ranking of the solutions.

It's important to consider both the short-term and long-term consequences of each proposed solution. A useful technique for this purpose is future scenario analysis. This method involves imagining different possible future scenarios following the implementation of a solution, considering both positive and negative outcomes. This approach can reveal potential problems or opportunities that may not be immediately evident.

Another valuable tool is the SWOT analysis (Strengths, Weaknesses, Opportunities, Threats). Applying this analysis to each proposed solution allows you to identify:

- Strengths: Intrinsic advantages of the solution

- Weaknesses: Limitations or disadvantages of the solution

- Opportunities: Potential benefits or positive developments

- Threats: Possible obstacles or external risks

Decision-making under uncertainty is a particular challenge in creative problem solving. In these cases, techniques such as sensitivity analysis can be useful. This method involves varying key parameters of the solution to see how the outcomes change. This can help identify which factors are most critical to the solution's success and where additional research or planning might be necessary.

Another technique for managing uncertainty is the Delphi method. This approach involves consulting a panel of experts in an anonymous and iterative manner. The experts provide their opinions, which are then aggregated and shared with the group. The process repeats, allowing experts to revise their assessments in light of the opinions of others. This method can be especially useful when addressing complex problems with many unknown variables.

It's also important to consider the ethical aspects of evaluating solutions. A useful framework for this is the utilitarian approach, which aims to maximize well-being for the greatest number of people.

However, it is crucial to balance this with considerations of fairness and justice.

Sometimes, the best solution can emerge from combining elements of different proposals. Being open to this kind of creative synthesis can lead to more robust and innovative solutions. Evaluating solutions is a complex process that requires a balance between objective analysis and intuitive judgment. By using a combination of objective criteria, analytical techniques, and ethical considerations, it is possible to identify the most promising solutions and develop a solid action plan to address the problem at hand.

Implementation and Feedback

Implementation is the moment of truth in creative problem-solving. This is where ideas are transformed into concrete actions and theoretical solutions are tested in the real world. To effectively move from idea to action, it is essential to have a clear and well-structured strategy. The first step in implementation is developing a detailed action plan. This plan should include:

- Clear and measurable objectives: What do you hope to achieve with the implementation of the solution?

- Milestones: What are the key steps in the implementation process?

- Timelines: When should each phase be completed?

- Resource allocation: What resources (human, financial, technological) are needed, and how will they be distributed?

- Responsibilities: Who is responsible for each aspect of the implementation?

- Success metrics: How will the success of the implementation be measured?

An effective technique for structuring this plan is the Gantt chart. This visual tool allows you to graphically represent the project phases over time, clearly showing dependencies between various activities and helping to identify potential bottlenecks. Another useful approach is the PDCA (Plan-Do-Check-Act) method, also known as the Deming cycle. This iterative method includes four stages:

- Plan: Develop the action plan
- Do: Implement the solution on a small scale
- Check: Evaluate the results
- Act: Make adjustments based on the results and repeat the cycle

This approach allows for testing and refining the solution incrementally, reducing the risks associated with large-scale changes. Continuous monitoring and evaluation are crucial during implementation. It is important to establish a regular feedback system that allows tracking progress, identifying issues promptly, and making necessary course corrections. This system might include:

- Regular team update meetings
- Visual dashboards showing progress towards key objectives
- Surveys or interviews with stakeholders to gather qualitative feedback
- Analysis of quantitative data related to established success metrics

Flexibility is essential during implementation. Even the best plans can encounter unforeseen obstacles or new opportunities. Being ready to adapt quickly based on feedback and new information is crucial for success.

Learning from mistakes is a fundamental part of the creative problem-solving process. When things don't go as planned, it's important to resist the temptation to find blame. Instead, view mistakes as opportunities for learning and improvement. Some useful techniques for learning from mistakes include:

- Project post-mortems: A structured review at the end of each major phase or the entire project to identify what worked well and what could be improved.

- "Fail fast, learn fast": This approach encourages quickly testing ideas on a small scale, learning from mistakes before making large investments.

- No-blame culture: Creating an environment where people feel safe to report problems and openly discuss mistakes.

Adapting solutions based on feedback is an art that requires balance. On one hand, it's important to be responsive and ready to make changes when necessary. On the other, it's crucial to avoid overreacting to every minor setback. Some strategies for navigating this balance include:

- Establishing clear criteria for making significant changes

- Using A/B testing techniques to evaluate the impact of small changes

- Maintaining a long-term vision, avoiding distractions from short-term fluctuations

Finally, it's important to celebrate successes along the way. Recognizing and celebrating the achievement of intermediate milestones can help maintain team motivation and create positive momentum. Implementation and feedback are critical phases in the creative problem-solving process. With careful planning, constant monitoring, a willingness to learn from mistakes, and the flexibility to adapt to change, it is possible to transform innovative ideas into effective and lasting solutions.

Chapter 10:
Lateral Thinking

"Creativity is intelligence having fun." - Albert Einstein

I magine being able to see solutions that no one else sees, to solve problems that seem impossible. Lateral thinking might be the key you've been searching for.

In this chapter, we will explore the transformative power of lateral thinking. You'll discover how this form of creative thinking can open up new perspectives, allowing you to tackle complex challenges in innovative ways. You'll learn practical techniques to break free from established mental patterns, generate original ideas, and see unexpected connections. Whether you're an entrepreneur seeking innovation, a professional facing complex problems, or simply someone looking to expand your mental horizons, the skills you'll develop here will enable you to approach the world with a more open and creative mind.

Beyond Linear Thinking

Lateral thinking, a concept introduced by Edward de Bono, represents a radically different approach to problem-solving and idea generation compared to traditional linear or vertical thinking. While vertical thinking proceeds logically and sequentially, lateral thinking seeks alternative and often counterintuitive paths.

Imagine the thinking process as a treasure hunt. Vertical thinking is like digging a hole deeper and deeper in the same spot, hoping to find the treasure. Lateral thinking, on the other hand, suggests digging in different spots, exploring areas that may initially seem unpromising.

A key feature of lateral thinking is its ability to challenge assumptions. Our minds often operate within established mental patterns, based on past experiences and acquired knowledge. While these patterns are useful in many situations, they can become limiting when dealing with new problems or seeking innovative solutions.

To illustrate this concept, consider the famous "nine dots problem." In this puzzle, you are asked to connect nine dots arranged in a 3x3 grid with four straight lines without lifting the pen from the paper. The solution requires you to "think outside the box" by literally extending the lines beyond the implicit boundaries formed by the dots. This example shows how our assumptions (in this case, that the lines must stay within the grid) can prevent us from seeing simple but unconventional solutions.

Lateral thinking encourages questioning these implicit assumptions. It's not about completely rejecting logical thinking but rather complementing it with a more flexible and creative approach. Here are some strategies to cultivate this mindset:

Problem Reframing:

Instead of accepting a problem as it is presented, look for different ways to define it. For example, if you are trying to increase product sales, you could reframe the problem from "How can we sell more?" to "How can we make our product indispensable to customers?"

Hypothesis Inversion:

Take the basic assumptions of a situation and invert them. For example, in a restaurant, instead of asking, "How can we serve customers faster?" you might ask, "What would happen if customers served themselves?" This could lead to innovative concepts like self-service restaurants or interactive dining experiences.

Random Analogies:

Connect your problem to a random object or concept. For instance, if you are trying to improve a business process, you might ask, "How would this process work if it were a beehive?" This could lead to ideas about efficiency, collaboration, and organizational structure.

Absurd "What Ifs":

Pose seemingly absurd questions and explore the consequences. "What if gravity worked in reverse for one hour each day?" This exercise stimulates your mind to consider completely new scenarios and can lead to surprising insights.

Perspective Shifting:

Approach the problem from someone else's point of view. How would a five-year-old see it? An alien newly arrived on Earth? A Renaissance artist? These different perspectives can reveal aspects of the problem you hadn't considered.

The goal of these strategies is not necessarily to find an immediate practical solution but to open the mind to new possibilities. Lateral thinking is a process of exploration where the journey is often more important than the immediate destination.

A fundamental aspect of lateral thinking is the suspension of judgment. When generating ideas, it's crucial to resist the urge to evaluate them immediately. Premature criticism can stifle creativity. Instead, create a mental environment where all ideas are welcome, no matter how strange or impractical they may initially seem. Often, the most bizarre ideas lead to the most innovative insights.

Lateral thinking is not an innate skill but an ability that can be developed with practice. Like a muscle that strengthens with exercise, your capacity for lateral thinking will improve with regular use. Start incorporating these strategies into your daily activities. You may be surprised at how, over time, your mind becomes more agile and creative in tackling challenges of all kinds.

Advanced Divergent Thinking Techniques

While lateral thinking provides the conceptual framework, divergent thinking offers practical tools for generating innovative ideas. In this section, we will explore advanced divergent thinking techniques that go beyond traditional brainstorming methods.

One particularly powerful technique is **Reverse Brainstorming**. Instead of looking for direct solutions to a problem, this method asks you to generate ways to cause or worsen the problem. The steps are:

1. Identify the problem, such as "How can we improve customer satisfaction?"

2. Reverse the problem: "How can we worsen customer satisfaction?"

3. Generate ideas for this reversed problem.

4. Reverse these ideas again to create solutions for the original problem.

This counterintuitive approach can reveal surprising insights. For example, if an idea to worsen customer satisfaction is "completely ignore their feedback," the inversion might lead to an innovative system for actively collecting and implementing customer feedback.

Another advanced technique is the **Modified Delphi Method**. Originally developed for technological forecasting, it can be adapted for creative idea generation:

1. Form a diverse panel of experts.

2. Present the problem and ask for anonymous solutions.

3. Compile and distribute all ideas to the group.

4. Ask each member to build on others' ideas or propose new ones.

5. Repeat the process multiple times, refining and combining ideas.

This method leverages diverse perspectives while avoiding groupthink, allowing for cross-fertilization of ideas in a non-judgmental environment.

The **Perfect Future Technique** is a powerful tool to overcome present constraints:

1. Imagine that the problem has been perfectly solved in the future.

2. Describe in detail what this ideal future looks like.

3. Work backwards from this ideal scenario, identifying the steps needed to achieve it.

This technique frees the mind from current limitations and can lead to bold and innovative solutions.

Method 635 is a structured technique for rapid idea generation:

1. Six participants sit around a table.

2. Each person writes three ideas on a sheet in five minutes.

3. The sheets are passed to the next person, who has five minutes to add three new ideas or elaborate on existing ones.

4. The process continues until each sheet has been passed to all participants.

In 30 minutes, this method can generate up to 108 ideas (6 participants x 3 ideas x 6 rounds).

The **Wanderer's Technique** harnesses the power of natural analogies:

1. Clearly define the problem.

2. Take a mental or physical "walk" in nature.

3. Observe natural elements closely (plants, animals, geological phenomena, etc.).

4. For each element, ask: "How does this solve problems similar to mine?"

5. Use these natural analogies to inspire solutions to your problem.

This technique can lead to innovative biomimetic solutions, like Velcro (inspired by burdock burrs) or bullet trains (inspired by the kingfisher's beak).

Applying these advanced techniques requires practice and an environment that fosters creative thinking. It's important to create a safe space where ideas, no matter how unconventional, can be freely expressed. Remember that the initial goal is quantity, not quality: generate as many ideas as possible without judging them immediately.

These techniques have been successfully applied in various fields. For example, IDEO, a renowned design company, has used variants of Reverse Brainstorming to develop innovative products. The Modified Delphi Method has been employed in technological forecasting and strategic planning projects at companies like IBM and Siemens.

In the field of social innovation, the Perfect Future Technique has been used to address complex challenges such as urban sustainability and access to education. Method 635 has found application in product innovation sessions at companies like 3M and Procter & Gamble.

Integrating these techniques into your problem-solving toolkit can radically transform how you approach challenges, both personal and professional. The key is consistent practice: the more you use these techniques, the better you will become at generating innovative ideas and seeing unexpected connections. Over time, divergent thinking will become second nature, allowing you to tackle any situation with creativity and mental flexibility.

Analogies and Metaphors in Problem Solving

Analogies and metaphors are powerful tools in lateral thinking and creative problem-solving. These rhetorical devices are not just linguistic embellishments but cognitive tools that allow us to understand and tackle complex situations through the lens of familiar experiences or seemingly unrelated concepts.

Using analogies in problem-solving is based on the principle that similar problems can have similar solutions, even if they occur in entirely different contexts. This approach allows us to transfer knowledge and strategies from one domain to another, opening new perspectives on seemingly unsolvable problems.

To effectively use analogies in problem-solving, follow these steps:

1. Clearly identify the problem you are trying to solve.
2. Abstract the problem to its essential elements, removing specific contextual details.
3. Look for situations or systems in other fields that present similar dynamics.
4. Analyze how these analogous problems were solved in their original context.
5. Transfer and adapt these solutions to your specific problem.

A classic example of analogical problem-solving is the development of the barcode system. The inventor, Norman Joseph Woodland, was inspired by Morse code, transferring the idea of representing information through lines and dots from the domain of communication to that of product identification.

Metaphors, on the other hand, allow us to conceptualize abstract or complex problems in more concrete and familiar terms. This can reveal aspects of the problem that might otherwise escape our attention.

To use metaphors in problem-solving:

1. Describe the problem in metaphorical terms. For example, you might see a business organization as an ecosystem, a production process as an assembly line, or a complex project as a mountain expedition.

2. Explore the implications of the metaphor. If your company is an ecosystem, what are the "key species"? How do the "resources" flow? What are the "predators" and "prey"?

3. Use the metaphor to generate new ideas. If thinking of a company as an ecosystem, you might consider concepts like symbiosis or evolutionary adaptation to develop new strategies.

4. Switch metaphors to gain different perspectives. Viewing the same problem through multiple metaphorical lenses can reveal surprising insights.

A powerful example of using metaphors in problem-solving comes from the field of molecular biology. When researchers were trying to understand how proteins fold into complex three-dimensional shapes, biochemist Cyrus Levinthal proposed the metaphor of the "golf course paradox". He imagined a protein as a golfer who must find the right hole among an astronomical number of possibilities, vividly illustrating the complexity of the problem and stimulating new research directions.

Analogies and metaphors can be particularly powerful when tackling problems in highly technical or specialized fields. They allow us to "translate" complex concepts into more accessible terms, facilitating communication and interdisciplinary collaboration.

However, it's important to be aware of the limits of this approach. No analogy or metaphor is perfect, and relying too heavily on a single analogy can lead to misleading conclusions. It's crucial to use multiple analogies and metaphors and remain open to reformulating or abandoning them when they are no longer useful.

To develop your ability to use analogies and metaphors in problem-solving:

1. Regularly practice creating analogies. Choose random objects or concepts and find similarities with the problem you are facing.

2. Cultivate diverse interests. The broader your knowledge in different fields, the richer your repertoire of potential analogies will be.

3. Challenge your metaphors. After formulating a metaphor, actively seek out its weaknesses and limitations.

4. Collaborate with people from different backgrounds. Their unique perspectives can bring forth analogies and metaphors you might never have considered.

Analogies and metaphors are not just linguistic tools but powerful cognitive strategies in creative problem-solving. By learning to effectively employ these techniques, you can unlock new perspectives and innovative solutions to complex problems.

Integrating Creativity and Analysis

While lateral thinking and creative techniques are powerful tools for generating innovative ideas, integrating these approaches with analytical thinking is crucial to transform ideas into practical and effective solutions. This section will explore how to balance and combine creative and analytical thinking to achieve the best results.

The integration process between creativity and analysis can be viewed as an iterative cycle:

1. Creative Idea Generation

2. Critical Analysis and Evaluation

3. Refinement and Development

4. Implementation and Testing

5. Reflection and Learning

In this cycle, creative and analytical phases alternate and inform each other. The key is to maintain a flexible mindset, smoothly transitioning between divergent and convergent thinking modes.

To critically evaluate the ideas generated through lateral thinking, consider the following criteria:

- Feasibility: Can the idea be realized with the available resources and technology?

- Relevance: How well does the idea address the original problem?

- Potential Impact: What could be the short-term and long-term effects?

- Scalability: Can the idea be expanded or adapted in the future?

- Risks and Challenges: What are the potential obstacles or negative side effects?

An effective method for applying these criteria is the weighted decision matrix. Assign a weight to each criterion based on its relative importance, then rate each idea on a numerical scale for each criterion. By multiplying the scores by the weights and summing the results, you can obtain an overall score for each idea.

However, it is important not to rely solely on quantitative methods. Intuition and qualitative judgment play a crucial role, especially when dealing with truly innovative ideas that may not fit well into conventional criteria.

To integrate lateral thinking into everyday decision-making:

- Practice "Creative Pauses": Before making a decision, take a moment to generate unconventional alternatives.

- Use the "Devil's Advocate" Technique: Deliberately challenge your assumptions and seek alternative perspectives.

- Apply "Hat Thinking": Consciously adopt different modes of thinking (creative, analytical, emotional, etc.) during the decision-making process.

- Implement "Rapid Prototyping": Quickly test ideas on a small scale before committing to long-term solutions.

- Practice "Retrospective Reflection": After implementing a solution, reflect on what worked, what didn't, and why.

Integrating creativity and analysis also requires an environment that supports both modes of thinking. This can include:

- Flexible physical spaces that encourage both creative collaboration and focused analytical work.

- An organizational culture that values both innovation and rigor.

- Decision-making processes that explicitly incorporate phases of divergent and convergent thinking.

- Continuous training that develops both creative and analytical skills.

Finally, it is important to recognize that integrating creativity and analysis is a skill that develops over time. It requires practice, patience, and the willingness to make mistakes and learn from them. With experience, you will become more adept at navigating between different modes of thinking, knowing when to push for more creative ideas and when to apply rigorous analysis.

Lateral thinking, when effectively integrated with critical analysis, can lead to solutions that are not only innovative but also practical and effective. This combination of creativity and rigor is what distinguishes truly exceptional problem solvers and successful innovators in any field.

Chapter 11:
Persuasive Communication

"If you would persuade, you must appeal to interest rather than intellect." - Benjamin Franklin

H ave you ever wished you could convince anyone of anything? The truth is, persuasion is an art, and you're about to become its master.

In this chapter, we will explore the fundamental techniques and strategies of persuasive communication. You will learn how to structure compelling arguments, balance appeals to logic, emotion, and ethics, and tailor your message to different types of audiences. Whether you are a leader aiming to inspire your team, an entrepreneur pitching your vision to potential investors, or simply someone looking to enhance your everyday communication skills, the competencies you develop here will enable you to convey your ideas with greater impact and effectiveness.

Structure of a Persuasive Argument

The foundation of effective persuasive communication is a solid and well-organized argumentative structure. The classical model of argumentation, which dates back to ancient Greece, provides a powerful and flexible framework for presenting your ideas convincingly.

This model comprises four main elements:

1. Thesis: The central claim you are trying to prove or the position you are advocating.

2. Evidence: The data, facts, and reasoning that support your thesis.

3. Refutation: Anticipating and responding to potential counter-arguments or objections.

4. Conclusion: Summarizing the main points and reinforcing your thesis.

The thesis is the heart of your argument. It must be clear, concise, and specific. An effective thesis not only states your position but also suggests why it is important or relevant. For example, instead of simply saying, "Recycling is important," you might assert, "Implementing a mandatory recycling program in our city will significantly reduce waste disposal costs and improve environmental quality for all residents."

Evidence forms the main body of your argument. Here, you present facts, statistics, examples, and logical reasoning that support your thesis. It is crucial that your evidence is relevant, accurate, and logically presented. Organize your evidence in order of importance or in a logical sequence that leads your audience towards your conclusion.

Refutation demonstrates that you have considered alternative perspectives and strengthens your argument by anticipating and addressing potential objections. This not only makes your argument more robust but also shows intellectual honesty and respect for your audience.

The conclusion should not merely be a summary but an opportunity to reinforce your main message and leave a lasting impression on your audience. You can do this by reconnecting to your initial thesis, emphasizing the importance or urgency of your position, or making a call to action.

The structure of a persuasive argument can vary slightly depending on the context. For example:

- In an academic setting: You might follow a more rigid structure, with a clear thesis statement at the beginning, followed by a review of existing literature, presentation of your evidence, discussion of the results, and a conclusion that ties everything together.

- In a business context, such as a sales presentation: You might start with a "hook" to capture attention, followed by presenting the problem your product or service solves (thesis), the benefits and features that make it unique (evidence), a comparison with alternatives (refutation), and a call to action (conclusion).

- In a public speech: You might use a more narrative structure, starting with a personal anecdote or engaging story that introduces your theme, developing your argument through examples and evidence, anticipating and responding to common objections, and concluding with an emotional appeal or an inspiring vision.

Regardless of the context, the key is to maintain a logical and coherent progression of ideas. Each point should flow naturally into the next, guiding your audience towards your conclusion in a convincing and engaging manner.

Remember, the structure is just the scaffolding of your argument. The true persuasive power comes from the content you fill this structure with and how you present it. In the following sections, we will explore how to enrich this structure with emotional, logical, and ethical appeals, and how to adapt it effectively to different types of audiences.

Appeal to Logic, Emotion, and Ethics

The Greek philosopher Aristotle identified three modes of persuasion: logos (logic), pathos (emotion), and ethos (character or credibility). When balanced effectively, these three elements form the foundation of powerful persuasive communication.

Logos refers to an appeal to reason and logic. It involves using facts, statistics, concrete examples, and deductive or inductive reasoning to support your argument. An appeal to logic is particularly effective when:

- Your audience consists of experts or professionals in the field.
- You are dealing with technical or scientific subjects.
- You need to overcome initial skepticism from your audience.

To use logos effectively:

- Present data and statistics clearly and in context.
- Use concrete examples to illustrate abstract concepts.
- Build logical arguments, clearly showing how your conclusions follow from the premises.

Pathos refers to an appeal to the audience's emotions. This does not mean manipulating feelings, but rather connecting your message to the audience's emotional experiences, values, and aspirations. An emotional appeal is especially powerful when:

- You want to inspire action or change.
- Your topic has significant personal or social implications.
- You are trying to create a sense of urgency or importance.

To use pathos effectively:

- Tell personal stories or anecdotes that the audience can relate to.

- Use vivid and descriptive language to evoke images and emotions.
- Connect your argument to the audience's values and concerns.

Ethos refers to your credibility as a speaker. It concerns the audience's perception of your character, competence, and reliability. A strong ethos is crucial because:

- People are more likely to be persuaded by someone they trust and respect.
- It establishes your authority on the subject.
- It creates a personal connection with the audience.

To strengthen your ethos:

- Establish your credentials and expertise on the subject.
- Show empathy and understanding for the audience's concerns.
- Be honest and transparent, acknowledging the limits of your knowledge or potential counterarguments.

Balancing these three elements is crucial for effective persuasion. An argument that relies solely on logic can seem cold and detached. Conversely, relying only on emotions can make your argument seem manipulative or lacking in substance. Without strong ethos, your audience may not trust you enough to be persuaded, regardless of the strength of your logical or emotional appeals.

The key is to tailor the mix of logos, pathos, and ethos to your specific audience and context. For example:

- **In a scientific presentation,** you might emphasize logos by using data and logical reasoning but also include elements of pathos to highlight the importance of the research, and ethos to establish your credibility in the field.

- **In a motivational speech,** you might rely more on pathos to inspire and motivate, but support it with logos (facts and concrete examples) and ethos (your personal experience and success) to add weight to your message.

- **In a business negotiation,** you might balance logos (financial data and projections) with ethos (your reputation and track record) and a touch of pathos (the shared vision of future success).

The goal is not to manipulate, but to communicate effectively and holistically. By utilizing all three elements, you can create an argument that not only convinces the mind but also touches the heart and earns the trust of your audience.

Effective Rhetorical Techniques

Rhetorical techniques are powerful tools that can elevate your persuasive communication from ordinary to memorable. Three of the most effective techniques are repetition, analogy, and rhetorical questions.

Repetition, when used skillfully, can emphasize key points and make them unforgettable. Martin Luther King Jr. masterfully employed this technique in his "I Have a Dream" speech, repeating the titular phrase eight times consecutively. Each repetition built on the previous one's emotion, creating a crescendo of rhetorical power.

To use repetition effectively:

- Choose a phrase or key idea that encapsulates your main message.

- Vary the phrase slightly with each repetition to maintain interest.

- Use repetition at pivotal moments in your speech or text to maximize impact.

Analogy helps explain complex or abstract concepts by comparing them to something familiar. Steve Jobs was known for his masterful use of analogies. When he introduced the iPod, he described it as "a thousand songs in your pocket," a simple yet powerful analogy that immediately captured the product's revolutionary essence.

To create effective analogies:

- Select something familiar and easily understandable for your audience.

- Ensure the analogy captures the essence of the concept you're explaining.

- Use the analogy to illuminate, not obscure; it should simplify, not complicate.

A rhetorical question is asked not to elicit an answer but to provoke thought or emphasize a point. John F. Kennedy's "Ask not what your country can do for you, ask what you can do for your country" is a classic example of how a rhetorical question can powerfully reframe a call to action.

To use rhetorical questions effectively:

- Formulate them in a way that guides the audience's thinking in the desired direction.

- Use them to introduce new topics or transitions between sections of your speech.

- Consider pausing after the question, allowing the audience time to reflect.

While these techniques can significantly enhance the impact of your message, it's essential to use them with moderation. Overuse can make your speech seem contrived or manipulative. The key is authenticity: rhetorical techniques should amplify your message, not replace it.

Moreover, the effectiveness of these techniques can vary depending on the context and audience. In a formal or academic setting, you might rely more heavily on analogies to explain complex concepts. In a motivational speech, repetition might play a more prominent role. In a debate, rhetorical questions might be particularly effective in challenging an opponent's positions.

The art of rhetoric lies in knowing when to use the right technique and seamlessly integrating it into your speech so that it strengthens your message without distracting from it. With practice, these techniques will become natural tools in your communicative arsenal, allowing you to articulate your ideas with greater clarity, impact, and persuasion.

Adapting to Your Audience

Knowing and understanding your audience is essential for effective persuasive communication. A message that resonates powerfully with one group might fall flat with another. The ability to tailor your message and style to different types of audiences can be the difference between successful and unsuccessful communication.

To know your audience, consider factors such as:

- Demographics: age, gender, education, profession
- Prior knowledge: what they already know about the topic
- Interests and values
- Potential concerns or objections
- Cultural and social context

These insights allow you to calibrate your message appropriately. For instance, if you're speaking to a group of experts, you can use technical terminology and delve into complex details. Conversely, with a general audience, you should simplify concepts and use analogies to make ideas more accessible.

Adapting your message goes beyond just the content. Consider also:

- Tone: formal or informal, serious or humorous
- Pace: fast and energetic or slow and reflective
- Body language: broad gestures or contained movements
- Use of visual aids: detailed charts or evocative images

A crucial element in adapting to your audience is managing objections and resistance. Anticipate possible objections from your audience and prepare to address them. Some effective strategies include:

- Acknowledgment and validation: Show that you understand the audience's concerns before countering them.
- Reframing: Present the objection from a different perspective that aligns better with your argument.
- Partial concession: Admit the validity of part of the objection, but demonstrate why your argument still holds.
- Counter-evidence: Provide data or examples that directly contradict the objection.

Remember, the goal is not to "win" a debate but to build a bridge of understanding with your audience. Sometimes, openly acknowledging the limitations of your argument can paradoxically increase your credibility.

Adapting to your audience is a dynamic process. Pay attention to verbal and non-verbal cues from your audience during communication. If you notice signs of confusion or disengagement, be ready to adjust your approach in real-time.

Finally, remember that authenticity is vital. Adapting to your audience doesn't mean completely changing your personality or values. It's about presenting your message in the most effective way for that particular group of people.

With practice, you'll develop the flexibility to adapt to different types of audiences while maintaining the integrity of your message. This skill will allow you to communicate persuasively in a variety of contexts, amplifying the impact of your ideas and enhancing your effectiveness as a communicator.

Chapter 12:
Ethics and Critical Thinking

"Ethics is knowing the difference between what you have a right to do and what is right to do." - Potter Stewart

I n this chapter, we will explore the crucial intersection between ethics and critical thinking. You will learn how to apply analytical reasoning skills to the complex moral issues that permeate our daily and professional lives. You will discover how to navigate ethical dilemmas, consider the broader implications of your decisions, and develop a solid and consistent personal ethical code. Whether you are a business leader facing tough decisions, a professional trying to balance conflicting responsibilities, or simply someone who wants to live a more ethical and mindful life, the skills you will develop here will equip you to handle moral challenges with greater clarity and confidence.

Foundations of Moral Philosophy

Moral philosophy provides the theoretical underpinnings for ethical reasoning. Three major ethical theories that have shaped Western thought are utilitarianism, deontology, and virtue ethics.

Utilitarianism, developed by philosophers like Jeremy Bentham and John Stuart Mill, argues that the right action is the one that produces the greatest happiness or well-being for the greatest number of people. According to this view, the consequences of an action are the sole criterion for judging its morality.

The strengths of utilitarianism include its conceptual simplicity and its focus on the concrete well-being of people. Additionally, it provides a clear framework for making decisions in complex situations, allowing for a comparison of different options based on their expected outcomes.

However, utilitarianism also has weaknesses. It can be challenging to predict and quantify all the consequences of an action, especially in the long term. Moreover, utilitarianism can sometimes justify actions that we intuitively consider immoral if they lead to a "greater good."

Deontology, primarily associated with philosopher Immanuel Kant, focuses on duty and moral rules. According to this theory, certain actions are intrinsically right or wrong, regardless of their consequences. Kant proposed the categorical imperative as a guiding principle: "Act only according to that maxim whereby you can at the same time will that it should become a universal law."

The strength of deontology lies in its provision of clear and universal moral principles that do not change based on circumstances. This can offer strong guidance in situations of moral pressure.

On the other hand, deontology can sometimes lead to counterintuitive results when applied rigidly. Additionally, it can be challenging to determine which moral rules should be considered universal.

Virtue ethics, which dates back to Aristotle, focuses on the character of the moral agent rather than on actions or their consequences. According to this view, the key question is not "What should I do?" but "What kind of person should I be?" Virtue ethics emphasizes qualities such as wisdom, courage, compassion, and integrity.

The advantage of this approach is that it acknowledges the complexity of moral situations and the importance of personal judgment. Moreover, it aligns well with the idea that ethics is not just about isolated decisions but about a way of living.

However, virtue ethics can be criticized for its lack of clear guidelines for action in specific situations. Additionally, it can be difficult to define and agree on which virtues should be cultivated.

In ethical decision-making, these theories can provide complementary perspectives. Utilitarianism encourages us to carefully consider the consequences of our actions. Deontology reminds us of the importance of consistent moral principles. Virtue ethics urges us to reflect on the kind of person we want to be and the qualities we want to cultivate.

In practice, many people adopt a hybrid approach, drawing from different theories depending on the situation. Ethical critical thinking involves the ability to apply these various frameworks flexibly, recognizing their strengths and weaknesses, and using them as tools to navigate the complex moral waters of real life.

Practical Analysis of Ethical Dilemmas:

Ethical dilemmas are situations where moral principles conflict, making it challenging to determine the right course of action. To navigate these murky waters, it's helpful to have a structured framework for analysis. An effective approach to analyzing ethical dilemmas can follow these steps:

1. **Identify the dilemma**: Clearly define the ethical conflict at hand.

2. **Gather the facts**: Ensure you have all relevant information.

3. **Identify the stakeholders**: Who will be affected by the decision?

4. **Consider the options**: List all possible courses of action.

5. **Apply ethical theories**: Consider how utilitarianism, deontology, and virtue ethics would evaluate each option.

6. **Evaluate the consequences**: Reflect on the short-term and long-term effects of each action.

7. **Examine the conflicting principles**: What values or duties are at stake?

8. **Seek precedents**: Have there been similar cases in the past? How were they resolved?

9. **Consult others**: Discuss the dilemma with trusted individuals to gain diverse perspectives.

10. **Make a decision**: Choose the action you believe is most ethically justifiable.

11. **Reflect**: After acting, reflect on the consequences and what you have learned.

Consider the classic example: the trolley problem. A runaway trolley is about to hit five people. You can divert the trolley onto another track, where it will kill one person. What do you do?

Applying our framework:

- **Identify the dilemma**: The choice is between inaction (letting five people die) and action (directly causing one person's death).

- **Gather the facts**: The number of lives at stake and the certainty of the consequences.

- **Identify the stakeholders**: The people on the tracks, you as the decision-maker, and potentially society at large.

- **Consider the options**: The primary options are to divert the trolley or not.

- **Apply ethical theories**: Utilitarianism would suggest diverting the trolley to save more lives. Deontology might oppose using one person as a means to save others. Virtue ethics might consider which action best reflects virtues like courage and compassion.

- **Evaluate the consequences**: Immediate consequences are clear, but also consider the psychological effects on yourself and the societal impact of normalizing such decisions.

- **Examine the conflicting principles**: The value of human life, the duty to help others, and the prohibition against actively killing.

- **Seek precedents**: This dilemma has been extensively discussed in philosophy, with various proposed resolutions.

- **Consult others**: Discussing this dilemma with others often reveals different moral intuitions and can lead to a deeper understanding.

- **Make a decision**: The final decision will depend on how you weigh the various factors and which ethical principles you find most important.

- **Reflect**: Reflecting on this dilemma can lead to broader insights about the value of life, the ethics of action versus inaction, and the limits of consequentialist reasoning.

This example illustrates how structured analysis can help dissect complex ethical dilemmas. However, it's important to recognize that many real-life dilemmas are less clear-cut and involve more nuances and uncertainties.

Considering multiple perspectives is crucial in ethical analysis. This includes not only different ethical theories but also the viewpoints of various stakeholders and diverse cultural backgrounds. This pluralistic approach can reveal considerations you might otherwise overlook and lead to more robust and ethically defensible decisions.

Social Responsibility and Critical Thinking

Social responsibility, both at the individual and collective level, is gaining increasing importance in our interconnected world. In this context, critical thinking becomes an essential tool for understanding and navigating the complex ethical implications of our actions.

On an individual level, social responsibility pushes us to consider the impact of our actions not only on ourselves but also on the community and the environment around us. This can manifest in seemingly simple daily choices, such as opting for ethical products, reducing our carbon footprint, or dedicating time to volunteering. However, critical thinking allows us to examine these choices more deeply. It prompts us to question whether our actions are genuinely making a difference or merely serving as a palliative for our conscience. It invites us to reflect on the real long-term consequences of our decisions and how we can maximize the positive impact of our choices.

When we shift our focus from the individual to the collective level, social responsibility takes on even broader dimensions, involving organizations, businesses, and governments. In this realm, critical thinking becomes essential for evaluating policies and practices in terms of their social and ethical impact. Consider a company that must balance profitability with environmental sustainability and employee well-being. Critical thinking in this case goes beyond a simple cost-benefit analysis. It encourages the consideration of complex scenarios, the identification of creative solutions that can benefit all stakeholders, and the anticipation of the long-term consequences of business decisions.

Ethical critical thinking in social contexts also challenges us to recognize and question problematic cultural norms. This process can be uncomfortable and difficult, as it asks us to critically examine accepted traditions and practices, recognize implicit biases in social structures, and propose more ethical and inclusive alternatives. It requires intellectual and moral courage, but it can lead to significant and positive social changes.

An illuminating example of how ethical critical thinking can trigger social transformations is the animal rights movement. By applying ethical reasoning to non-human animals, philosophers and activists have challenged existing social norms, leading to significant changes in laws and practices related to animal welfare. This movement has demonstrated how critical thinking can expand our circle of moral consideration, pushing us to reconsider ethical relationships we have taken for granted.

Another example is the evolution of the concept of corporate social responsibility (CSR). Critical thinking has pushed companies beyond the mere pursuit of financial profit, encouraging them to incorporate environmental and social considerations into their business strategies. This paradigm shift is redefining the role of businesses in society, showing how critical thinking can influence even the most entrenched economic structures.

However, navigating issues of social responsibility also requires the ability to manage complexity and ambiguity. We rarely encounter simple or universally "right" answers. Critical thinking helps us recognize the complexity of social issues, avoid simplistic or dogmatic solutions, and remain open to new information and perspectives. It teaches us that social responsibility and ethical thinking are continuous processes, not final destinations.

In conclusion, integrating critical thinking into our understanding of social responsibility allows us to make more informed, ethical, and impactful decisions. It helps us see beyond superficial appearances and consider the deeper implications of our actions, both as individuals and as members of a global society. In a rapidly changing world, this capacity for ethical critical thinking becomes not only an advantage but a necessity for navigating the complex moral waters of our time.

Developing a Personal Code of Ethics

Developing a personal code of ethics is a deeply reflective process that requires honest introspection and careful consideration of one's core values. This code serves as a moral compass, guiding us through the complex ethical decisions we face daily.

The starting point for developing a personal code of ethics is identifying your core values. These may include concepts such as honesty, compassion, justice, responsibility, or respect for individual autonomy. Reflect on the experiences that have shaped your worldview, the people you admire, and the principles you consider inviolable. This self-exploration process can take time and may be facilitated through journaling, meditation, or in-depth discussions with trusted individuals.

Once you've identified your core values, the next step is to articulate them into clear, applicable guiding principles. These principles should be specific enough to provide practical guidance, yet flexible enough to adapt to various situations. For example, if honesty is a core value, a guiding principle might be: "I commit to telling the truth, even when it's uncomfortable, but with compassion and consideration for others' well-being."

It's important to recognize that values can sometimes conflict with each other. A robust ethical code should provide a framework for navigating these conflicts. You might establish a hierarchy of values or develop criteria for balancing conflicting principles. For instance, you might decide that preventing harm always takes precedence over absolute truthfulness.

The process of developing a personal code of ethics is not a purely theoretical exercise. It's essential to test your principles against real-life scenarios. Consider how you would apply your code in difficult situations you've faced in the past or might encounter in the future.

This exercise can reveal gaps or contradictions in your code, allowing you to refine it further.

Applying your ethical code in everyday situations requires practice and awareness. You might find it helpful to create visual reminders of your key principles or establish regular moments for ethical reflection. Over time, adherence to your code will become more natural, informing your decisions at an almost intuitive level.

However, it's crucial to remain flexible and open to growth. Your ethical code shouldn't be a static document, but rather a living entity that evolves with you. New experiences, knowledge, and perspectives may lead you to reconsider and refine your principles over time.

A personal code of ethics doesn't exist in a vacuum. It's important to consider how your principles align with or conflict with the social norms and professional expectations that surround you. This doesn't necessarily mean conforming to these norms, but rather being aware of potential tensions and preparing to address them constructively.

Finally, remember that having an ethical code doesn't automatically guarantee ethical behavior. The real challenge lies in living up to your principles, especially when doing so is difficult or uncomfortable. There will be times when you fail to meet your standards. What's important is to recognize these failures, learn from them, and commit to doing better in the future.

Developing and applying a personal code of ethics is an ongoing journey of self-discovery and growth. It's a process that requires courage, honesty, and perseverance. But it's also a deeply rewarding process that can lead to a more authentic, consistent, and morally satisfying life. In a world often characterized by moral ambiguity, a well-developed personal code of ethics can provide a sense of direction and purpose, allowing us to navigate ethical challenges with greater clarity and confidence.

Chapter 13:
Critical Thinking in Everyday Life

"Life is the sum of all your choices." - Albert Camus

I magine facing every challenge of daily life with the clarity of a philosopher and the precision of a scientist. This chapter will show you how. We will explore how to integrate critical thinking into the various facets of everyday life. You will discover how to apply the analytical skills you have developed to make more informed decisions, manage your finances with greater wisdom, improve your interpersonal relationships, and make more conscious choices regarding your health and well-being. The goal is to transform critical thinking from an abstract exercise into a practical and powerful tool that you can use daily to enhance the quality of your life.

Making Informed Decisions

Decision-making is at the heart of nearly every aspect of our daily lives, from trivial choices like what to have for breakfast to life-changing decisions that alter the course of our existence. Applying critical thinking to this process can significantly enhance the quality of our decisions and, consequently, the quality of our lives.

An effective model for critical thinking-based decision-making might follow these steps:

1. Clearly identify the decision to be made

2. Gather relevant information

3. Identify possible options

4. Evaluate the evidence for and against each option

5. Consider the potential consequences of each choice

6. Make the decision

7. Reflect on the outcome and learn from the experience

This model can be applied to decisions of any magnitude. For example, consider a daily decision like choosing what to eat for dinner. Instead of relying on habit or impulse, you could:

1. Identify the decision: "What should I have for dinner tonight?"

2. Gather information: Check what you have in the fridge, consider your budget, the time available for cooking, and any dietary restrictions.

3. Identify options: Cooking at home, ordering takeout, or eating out.

4. Evaluate the evidence: Consider the pros and cons of each option in terms of health, cost, time, and taste.

5. Consider the consequences: How will it affect your weekly budget? How will you feel after the meal?

6. Make the decision: Choose the option that best balances all the factors considered.

7. Reflect: After the meal, assess whether you are satisfied with your choice and what you might do differently next time.

This approach might seem excessive for a daily decision, but with practice, it will become a quick and almost automatic process that can lead to more satisfying choices aligned with your long-term goals.

For more significant decisions, such as changing jobs or moving to a new city, this model becomes even more valuable. It allows you to systematically consider all relevant aspects, avoiding impulsive decisions or those based on incomplete information.

Critical thinking can enhance the quality of decisions in various ways:

- Reduces cognitive biases: Helps you see beyond prejudices and unexamined assumptions.

- Encourages diverse information sources: Expands your perspective by actively seeking information from different sources.

- Assesses information credibility: Helps you distinguish between facts, opinions, and propaganda.

- Considers long-term consequences: Encourages thinking about long-term outcomes, not just immediate benefits.

- Clarifies decision rationale: Allows you to articulate the reasons for your decisions, making you more confident in your choices and better able to explain them to others.

However, it's important to remember that critical thinking does not eliminate uncertainty or guarantee perfect outcomes. Its value lies in making you more aware, informed, and reflective in your decision-making process, increasing the likelihood of making choices that align with your long-term values and goals.

Incorporating this approach into your daily decisions requires practice and patience. Start by consciously applying it to one or two decisions a day. Over time, it will become second nature, enabling you to navigate the complexities of everyday life with greater clarity and confidence.

Managing Personal Finances

Managing personal finances is an area where critical thinking can have a profound and lasting impact on the quality of life. In a world saturated with complex financial products, conflicting advice, and often misleading information, the ability to think critically becomes an invaluable asset.

Applying critical thinking to budgeting begins with an objective assessment of your financial situation. This means carefully examining income and expenses, identifying spending patterns, and pinpointing areas for potential improvement. A critical approach urges you to question your financial habits: Is that recurring expense really necessary? Is your savings rate adequate for your long-term goals?

In budgeting, critical thinking helps distinguish between wants and needs, prioritize expenses, and identify opportunities for optimization. It encourages you to consider future scenarios and prepare for unforeseen events, promoting more resilient financial management.

When it comes to investments, critical thinking is essential for navigating the sea of available financial information. It allows you to:

- Critically evaluate financial information sources, distinguishing between unbiased advice and disguised marketing.

- Analyze past investment performance in the appropriate context, recognizing that past results do not guarantee future performance.

- Understand your risk profile and how it aligns with different types of investments.

- Recognize and mitigate cognitive biases that can influence investment decisions, such as confirmation bias or loss aversion.

A crucial aspect of critical thinking in personal finance is evaluating financial information. In an age of information overload, developing the ability to discern reliable information from background noise is essential. This involves:

- Checking the credentials and interests of financial information sources.

- Seeking concrete evidence to support financial claims.

- Being skeptical of promises of high returns with low risks.

- Considering multiple perspectives before making significant financial decisions.

Critical thinking can also help you avoid common financial mistakes, such as:

- Herd mentality: Instead of blindly following popular investment trends, a critical thinker will objectively assess the merits of each opportunity.

- Analysis paralysis: Critical thinking helps find a balance between gathering sufficient information and acting in a timely manner.

- Present bias: It encourages consideration of the long-term implications of financial decisions, rather than focusing solely on immediate benefits.

A practical application of critical thinking in personal finance might be evaluating a significant purchase, such as a house. A critical approach would lead you to consider not only the purchase price but also maintenance costs, tax implications, appreciation potential, and how the purchase aligns with your long-term life goals.

Finally, critical thinking in personal finance involves continuous self-assessment. Regularly reflecting on your financial decisions, learning from successes and mistakes, and being willing to adapt your strategies based on new information or changes in life circumstances are all crucial aspects of sound and mindful financial management.

In conclusion, applying critical thinking to personal finance does not guarantee financial success, but it provides the tools to make more informed decisions, manage risks more effectively, and align your financial choices with your values and life goals. It is an ongoing process of learning and adaptation that can lead to greater financial security and peace of mind.

Interpersonal Relationships and Communication

Interpersonal relationships and effective communication are fundamental to our well-being and success in nearly every aspect of life. Applying critical thinking to this domain can significantly enhance the quality of our interactions and the depth of our connections.

In the context of communication, critical thinking first helps us to listen actively. Instead of mentally formulating our response while the other person is still speaking, a critical approach encourages us to truly focus on what is being said, strive to understand the other person's point of view, and identify any assumptions or biases in their (and our) words.

This form of active and critical listening can greatly improve empathy. It allows us to look beyond superficial words and try to understand the underlying emotions, motivations, and experiences that influence the other person's behavior and communication. This doesn't necessarily mean agreeing with everything but rather striving to truly understand before judging or responding.

When formulating our responses, critical thinking helps us to be more precise and effective. It urges us to carefully consider our words, evaluate their potential impact, and choose the best way to express our ideas based on the context and the interlocutor. This can lead to clearer communication, reducing misunderstandings and improving the overall quality of our interactions.

When it comes to resolving conflicts, critical thinking becomes an especially valuable tool. It allows us to:

- Objectively analyze the situation, separating facts from emotions and interpretations.

- Identify the true causes of the conflict, going beyond superficial symptoms.

- Consider multiple perspectives and potential solutions.

- Evaluate the short- and long-term consequences of different actions.

- Negotiate solutions that take into account the interests of all parties involved.

A critical approach to conflict resolution also encourages us to question our assumptions and be open to changing our position in light of new information or perspectives. This attitude can transform potential clashes into opportunities for growth and mutual understanding.

Critical thinking is also crucial for evaluating relational dynamics more objectively. It helps us recognize behavioral patterns, identify healthy and toxic relationships, and make informed decisions about how to invest our time and emotional energy. We can use it to critically examine our expectations in relationships, assess whether they are realistic and healthy, and adjust them if necessary.

Moreover, critical thinking can enhance our ability to give and receive feedback. It pushes us to provide feedback that is specific, constructive, and based on concrete observations rather than personal judgments. Similarly, when receiving feedback, a critical approach helps us to evaluate it objectively, distinguish between valid and unfounded criticisms, and use the information for our personal improvement.

It's important to note that applying critical thinking to interpersonal relationships doesn't mean being cold or detached. On the contrary, it's about combining rational analysis with emotional intelligence to create more authentic, empathetic, and meaningful interactions.

Finally, critical thinking in relationships helps us to recognize and challenge stereotypes and prejudices, both our own and those of others. It encourages us to see people as complex individuals rather than through the lens of simplified categories. This can lead to more inclusive relationships and a deeper understanding of human diversity.

Integrating critical thinking into our interpersonal relationships and communication can lead to more authentic, empathetic, and fulfilling interactions. It allows us to navigate the complexities of human relationships with greater awareness and wisdom, contributing to deeper and more meaningful connections in our personal and professional lives.

Health and Wellness

Applying critical thinking to decisions about health and personal well-being is essential, especially given the abundance of often contradictory or misleading medical information available today. This approach can help you make informed decisions and manage your health more effectively.

When making health decisions, start by evaluating the sources of information. Not all sources are reliable, so it's important to differentiate between solid scientific evidence, personal opinions, and commercial interests. This involves:

- Checking the credentials of experts cited.
- Looking for peer-reviewed studies rather than relying on individual testimonials or anecdotes.
- Being skeptical of sensational claims or "miracle cures."
- Considering potential conflicts of interest in the sources of information.

Critical thinking encourages you to ask detailed questions when assessing treatment options:

- What are the risks and benefits of this treatment?
- Are there alternative treatments? How do they compare in terms of effectiveness and risks?
- What scientific evidence supports this approach?
- How does this treatment align with my personal values and preferences?

This method is particularly useful for preventive medicine and lifestyle choices. Critical thinking helps you evaluate the effectiveness of various diets, exercise routines, or stress management techniques. It allows you to move beyond fleeting trends and adopt habits based on solid scientific evidence tailored to your needs.

Communication with healthcare professionals also benefits from critical thinking. It encourages you to be an informed and proactive patient by:

- Preparing questions before medical visits.
- Asking for clarifications when needed.
- Discussing the pros and cons of different treatments openly.
- Being open to seeking a second opinion for significant decisions.

For mental wellness, critical thinking supports self-reflection and personal growth. It helps you to:

- Identify negative or unhelpful thought patterns.
- Assess your emotional reactions objectively.
- Develop evidence-based strategies to manage stress and anxiety.

- Recognize when professional help is necessary.

However, it is essential to balance critical analysis with attentiveness to your body and intuition. Critical thinking should not result in overanalyzing or ignoring important physical or emotional signals. Instead, it should enhance your awareness of your body's and mind's needs.

A critical approach to wellness also means considering health holistically. Rather than focusing only on specific symptoms, think about how different aspects of your life—such as diet, exercise, stress, relationships, and environment—interact to affect your overall well-being.

Lastly, critical thinking is crucial for understanding health policies and the healthcare system. It helps you grasp your rights as a patient, evaluate health insurance options critically, and make informed decisions about public health issues that might affect you and your community.

Applying critical thinking to health and wellness decisions doesn't mean becoming cynical or distrustful of modern medicine. Instead, it involves being an active and informed participant in managing your health. This approach can lead to better decisions, improved adherence to necessary treatments, and ultimately, a higher quality of life and overall well-being.

Chapter 14:
Critical Thinking in the Digital World

"We live in a digital world, but we are analog creatures." - Omar Ahmad

I n a world where virtual reality merges with the physical, how can you discern the real from the fake, the valuable from the trivial? This chapter will guide you through the intricacies of the digital landscape, equipping you with tools to navigate the information age with confidence and wisdom. We will explore how to apply critical thinking to social media, online security, interactions with artificial intelligence, and advanced digital literacy. The aim is to transform you from a passive consumer of digital content into an active and discerning user, capable of making the most of the digital world's opportunities while avoiding its pitfalls.

Navigating Social Media with Critical Thinking

In the world of social media, where stories intertwine with complex algorithms and opaque business models, critical thinking needs to go beyond just fact-checking. We must understand the underlying structures shaping our online experience.

First, consider the attention economy driving social media. Every platform is designed not just to inform or connect but primarily to capture and monetize your attention. This economic imperative deeply influences the type and presentation of content you see. Critically analyze how this business model affects your perception of reality and social interactions.

Personalization algorithms, while providing tailored content, also create what Eli Pariser calls a "filter bubble." These information bubbles are not just echo chambers but complex ecosystems that reinforce certain thought patterns while excluding others. The challenge is not just exposing yourself to different opinions but understanding how these algorithmic systems actively shape your worldview.

Misinformation on social media goes beyond simple fake news. It includes sophisticated techniques like astroturfing, where orchestrated campaigns mimic genuine grassroots movements, and sentiment manipulation, where bots and fake accounts influence public opinion. Recognizing these patterns requires not only skepticism but also an understanding of the amplification and virality mechanisms unique to each platform.

Critical analysis of social media content must also consider the broader geopolitical and cultural context. The narratives you encounter online are often the product of complex dynamics of soft power and information warfare. Develop the ability to recognize how global events and geopolitical tensions manifest and are manipulated within the social media ecosystem.

To navigate this landscape effectively:

1. Study the business models and algorithms of the platforms you use. Understand how they generate profit and how this affects what you see.

2. Use data analysis tools to critically examine your social media interactions. Analyze your engagement patterns to identify implicit biases.

3. Practice "distant reading" of social media. Instead of focusing solely on individual content, observe broader patterns of how information spreads and evolves over time.

4. Develop skills in OSINT (Open Source Intelligence) to verify and contextualize the information you encounter.

5. Consider the psychological impact of social media use. Critically analyze how it affects your mental well-being, relationships, and productivity.

Finally, reflect on your active role in the social media ecosystem. Every interaction you have contributes to the shaping of the information environment. Consider the ethical responsibility of your online actions and how you can contribute to a healthier, more informed public discourse.

Navigating social media with critical thinking in this era requires a multidisciplinary approach that integrates technological understanding, psychological awareness, and sociopolitical analysis. Only through this comprehensive lens can we hope to maintain our intellectual autonomy in the increasingly complex digital landscape.

Online Security and Privacy

The "privacy paradox" highlights the gap between expressed concerns about privacy and actual online behavior. This phenomenon reveals the complexity of privacy decisions in the digital age. A critical analysis of your data-sharing choices is essential: are they truly aligned with your values, or are they influenced by immediate gratification and social pressures? This reflection requires a deep examination of the motivations behind your online actions.

The business model of "surveillance capitalism," as theorized by Shoshana Zuboff, is based on the large-scale extraction and monetization of personal data. Every online interaction feeds this system, with long-term implications for individual autonomy and democracy. Understanding this mechanism is key to navigating the digital landscape consciously. Consider how your online activities contribute to this ecosystem and reflect on the potential future consequences.

When it comes to online security, three areas need particular attention:

1. **Quantum Computing and Cryptography**: The impact of quantum computing on current cryptographic measures represents a significant challenge. Current security measures may become obsolete, risking long-term data protection. It is essential to stay updated on developments in this field and consider adopting post-quantum cryptography when available.

2. **Ethical and Security Implications of the Internet of Things (IoT)**: The convenience of always-connected devices must be balanced with vulnerability risks. Critically analyze each IoT device you introduce into your environment: what data does it collect? How are these data transmitted and stored? What are the potential access points for malicious actors?

3. **Digital Security in Geopolitical Dynamics**: Digital vulnerabilities can be exploited in international conflicts, turning personal devices into potential attack vectors. Stay informed about geopolitical tensions and consider how they might affect your digital security.

To make informed decisions about sharing personal data, adopt a systematic approach:

- **Cost-Benefit Analysis**: Critically evaluate the value you receive in exchange for your data. This assessment should go beyond immediate benefits and consider long-term implications. For example, is the convenience of a voice assistant worth the risk of having a constant listening device in your home?

- **Data Mapping**: Create a detailed map of your digital data. Where is it stored? Who has access? How is it used? This visualization can reveal vulnerabilities and dependencies.

Consider using data visualization tools to make this process more effective.

- **Scenario Planning**: Imagine different future scenarios regarding the use of your data. How might they be used in various political, economic, or social contexts? This exercise can help you foresee and mitigate potential future risks.

- **Ethical Audit**: Regularly evaluate the privacy policies of the platforms you use. Do they align with your ethical values? How have they changed over time? This process should include reviewing privacy settings and critically assessing the permissions granted to applications.

Your privacy choices have implications beyond your personal sphere. Consider how they affect the privacy of others in your social or professional network. For instance, sharing a group photo might inadvertently expose the location or activities of other people. Reflect on how your actions contribute to shaping social norms around privacy.

The concept of "nothing to hide" is often used to justify mass surveillance, but it overlooks the complex power dynamics involved in data collection and use. Privacy isn't just about hiding "bad" information but about maintaining personal autonomy and the freedom of thought and expression. Consider how a lack of privacy could affect your behavior, choices, and freedom of expression in the long term.

Finally, remember that online security and privacy are ongoing processes, not final destinations. Threats constantly evolve, as do the technologies to counter them. Maintain a proactive approach by regularly informing yourself about new threats and best security practices. Develop the habit of reviewing and updating your security and privacy practices regularly.

Artificial Intelligence and Critical Thinking

The advent of artificial intelligence (AI) is radically redefining our relationship with technology and information. In this context, critical thinking assumes an even more crucial role, requiring a deeper and more nuanced understanding of AI's implications in our daily lives and society in general.

AI, in its various forms—from machine learning to more advanced deep learning systems—is permeating every aspect of our digital lives. Recommendation systems that influence our consumption choices, virtual assistants that manage our schedules, predictive models that guide decisions in healthcare and finance: all these are examples of how AI is shaping our decision-making environment.

One of the main challenges in the era of AI is the "black box" problem. Many AI algorithms, especially those based on deep neural networks, operate in ways that are difficult to interpret, even for their creators. This raises fundamental questions about accountability and transparency. How can we critically evaluate decisions made by systems we do not fully understand?

To address this challenge, new forms of algorithmic literacy need to be developed. This doesn't necessarily mean understanding the technical details of every algorithm but rather acquiring a conceptual understanding of how AI systems work, their strengths and weaknesses, and how they can be influenced by biases in training data or design.

A critical approach to AI also requires a constant evaluation of its ethical and social impacts. Consider, for example, the use of AI in predictive justice systems or hiring processes. How can we ensure that these systems do not perpetuate or even amplify existing biases? Here, critical thinking must extend beyond technical analysis to include considerations of social justice and equity.

When evaluating AI decisions and outcomes, it is crucial to maintain a healthy skepticism. This does not mean rejecting AI conclusions outright, but rather:

- Critically examining the input data: What data was used to train the system? Is it representative? Does it contain implicit biases?

- Assessing the application context: Is AI appropriate for this specific task or decision? Are there crucial human factors that might be overlooked?

- Considering limitations: What are the known limits of the system? How does it handle uncertainty or unforeseen cases in its training?

- Analyzing impacts: What are the potential consequences of AI-based decisions, both short-term and long-term?

Effective collaboration with AI systems requires a delicate balance between trust and vigilance. On one hand, we must be open to the benefits AI can bring in terms of efficiency and accuracy. On the other, we must maintain our decision-making autonomy and the ability to override when necessary.

Strategies for effective collaboration with AI include:

- Developing an understanding of AI's strengths and weaknesses in your specific field.

- Practicing critical interpretation of AI results, contextualizing them with your experience and domain knowledge.

- Maintaining a "human-in-the-loop" approach, where AI supports but does not completely replace human judgment.

- Actively participating in the dialogue on ethical AI development in your sector or community.

Finally, it is important to recognize that AI is changing not only how we make decisions but also how we think. Constant exposure to recommendation systems and AI assistants may subtly but profoundly influence our cognitive processes. A critical thinker in the AI era must be aware of these influences and actively engage in maintaining and cultivating their independent reasoning skills.

Navigating the AI era requires evolved critical thinking, combining technical understanding, ethical awareness, and continuous reflection on the role of technology in our lives and society. Only through this approach can we hope to harness the potential of AI while maintaining our autonomy and fundamental human values.

Advanced Digital Literacy

Digital literacy goes far beyond the mere ability to use devices and digital platforms. It involves developing a deep and critical understanding of the digital ecosystem, its dynamics, and its impact on society and individuals.

A fundamental aspect of advanced digital literacy is the ability to decode and critically analyze the architecture of online information. This includes understanding how search and recommendation algorithms influence what we see and how we see it. For example, it's essential to recognize how SEO (Search Engine Optimization) can manipulate the visibility and perception of online information, often favoring content optimized for engagement rather than accuracy or relevance.

Critically evaluating digital information sources requires a set of advanced skills:

- Data Provenance Analysis: Don't just check the author or website, but explore the data provenance chain. Who collected the original data? How was it processed and interpreted?

- Methodology Verification: For content based on research or analysis, critically examine the methodology used. Are the methods appropriate? Is the sample representative? Are the conclusions justified by the data?

- Contextualizing Information: Consider how the broader context—social, political, economic—can influence the presentation and interpretation of information.

- Recognizing Disinformation Patterns: Familiarize yourself with advanced information manipulation tactics, such as the use of bots to amplify certain narratives or astroturfing techniques to simulate grassroots consensus.

- Critical Data Visualization Analysis: Develop the ability to read and interpret complex graphs and visualizations, recognizing how visual presentation can be manipulated to influence perception.

Another crucial aspect of advanced digital literacy is understanding the attention economy that drives much of the digital ecosystem. This involves recognizing how platform and application design is often optimized to maximize engagement and data collection, sometimes at the expense of user well-being or information quality.

Managing one's online presence requires sophisticated awareness of the long-term implications of digital actions. This goes beyond merely curating your online reputation, including:

- Understanding Digital Data Persistence: Recognize that information shared online can persist indefinitely, even after attempts to delete it.

- Managing Distributed Digital Identity: Develop strategies for managing your identity across multiple platforms, recognizing how different parts of your online presence contribute to your overall digital identity.

- Navigating Tensions Between Authenticity and Privacy: Balance the desire for authentic expression with the need to protect your privacy and online security.

- Understanding Legal and Ethical Implications: Familiarize yourself with data privacy laws and the terms of service of the platforms you use, recognizing the ethical implications of your online actions.

Advanced digital literacy also includes the ability to effectively navigate and contribute to online communities. This requires:

- Recognizing Online Group Dynamics: Understand how online interactions can amplify certain behaviors and how social norms develop in digital spaces.

- Ethical Participation: Develop the ability to contribute constructively to online discussions, recognizing the impact of your words in a digital context.

- Managing Dissent and Conflict: Learn to navigate disagreements and conflicts productively in online environments, where the nuances of face-to-face communication are absent.

Finally, an often overlooked but crucial aspect of advanced digital literacy is understanding the environmental impact of digital technologies. This includes awareness of the energy consumption of data centers, the carbon footprint associated with the use of digital devices, and the ecological implications of the rapid replacement cycle of technological devices.

Chapter 15:
The Future of Critical Thinking

"The best way to predict the future is to create it." - Alan Kay

W hat will the world be like in 10, 20, or 50 years? No one knows for sure, but with critical thinking, you'll be ready to face any future.

This chapter will explore emerging trends in critical thinking and how these will impact various aspects of society. We will examine the crucial role of education in cultivating these skills and how critical thinking can help us tackle global challenges. Finally, we will discuss the importance of maintaining a mindset of continuous learning in a rapidly changing world. The goal is to equip you with the tools to adapt and thrive in an uncertain future, using critical thinking as your

Emerging Trends in Critical Thinking

Critical thinking is evolving to address the increasing complexity of the modern world. One emerging trend is systemic thinking, which focuses on the interconnections between various elements rather than analyzing them in isolation. This approach is particularly relevant for tackling complex problems like climate change or global economic crises, where linear solutions often fail.

Advanced metacognition, or "thinking about thinking," is gaining importance. This practice goes beyond simple awareness of one's mental processes, including sophisticated strategies to optimize one's thinking in real-time. Techniques such as "cognitive calibration" help assess the accuracy of one's knowledge and decisions, enhancing the quality of critical thinking.

The integration of critical thinking with emotional intelligence is emerging as a promising field. Recognizing and managing emotions during the reasoning process can lead to more balanced decisions and better communication of critical ideas.

These trends are influencing various fields. In education, there is a movement towards curricula that emphasize systemic thinking and metacognition, preparing students for a world of increasing complexity. In business, companies are adopting problem-solving approaches based on systemic thinking to navigate volatile and interconnected markets. In politics, the ability to critically analyze large amounts of data and understand complex systems is becoming increasingly crucial for effective policy-making.

To stay updated on these developments:

- Follow academic publications and conferences dedicated to critical thinking.
- Join online communities of critical thinking practitioners.
- Regularly experiment with new thinking techniques and reflect on their effectiveness.
- Seek opportunities to apply these new forms of critical thinking in your specific field.

The future of critical thinking will require greater cognitive flexibility and the ability to integrate different modes of thinking. Developing these skills will not only prepare you for future challenges but also enable you to actively contribute to shaping that future.

Education and Critical Thinking

Integrating critical thinking into school curricula is essential for preparing future generations to face the challenges of a rapidly evolving world. However, this requires a radical rethinking of traditional educational approaches.

The importance of this integration lies in its ability to develop adaptable and resilient minds. In an era where information is abundant but not always reliable, the ability to analyze, evaluate, and synthesize becomes crucial. Critical thinking is not just an academic skill but an essential life skill.

New approaches to teaching critical thinking are emerging:

- Problem-Based Learning: Students tackle complex real-world scenarios, applying critical thinking to find solutions.

- Structured Debates: Students are encouraged to examine issues from multiple perspectives, developing evidence-based arguments.

- Guided Metacognition: Teachers facilitate students' reflection on their own thinking processes, promoting self-awareness and self-regulation.

- Technological Integration: The use of simulations and virtual reality to create immersive learning environments that stimulate critical thinking.

- Formative Assessment: Focusing on the thinking process rather than just outcomes, providing continuous feedback to improve critical thinking skills.

These approaches require a paradigm shift in the educator's role, from knowledge dispenser to facilitator of critical learning.

Lifelong learning of critical thinking goes beyond formal education. Strategies to cultivate these skills include:

- Deliberate Practice: Regularly engage in critical thinking exercises, gradually increasing complexity.

- Critical Reading: Actively analyze texts from various genres, identifying arguments, evidence, and biases.

- Interdisciplinary Discussions: Participate in debates on topics intersecting multiple disciplines to develop a broader perspective.

- Structured Self-Reflection: Keep a critical thinking journal, regularly analyzing your decision-making and reasoning processes.

- Mentorship and Peer Learning: Seek feedback from experienced mentors and engage in critical discussions with peers.

Critical thinking education must also consider emerging ethical challenges. With the advent of technologies like artificial intelligence, it is crucial to develop a robust ethical framework to guide the application of critical thinking.

Moreover, critical thinking education must be inclusive, recognizing and valuing diverse cultural perspectives and ways of thinking. This approach not only enriches the learning process but also prepares students to operate in a globally interconnected world.

Measuring the effectiveness of critical thinking education remains a challenge. New assessment methods are emerging, focusing not only on problem-solving ability but also on cognitive flexibility and the capacity to quickly learn and unlearn.

Finally, critical thinking education must extend beyond formal institutions. Organizations, communities, and individuals must recognize the value of lifelong learning and create opportunities for the continuous development of these essential skills.

Critical Thinking and Global Change

Critical thinking is proving to be an indispensable tool in addressing the complex global challenges of our time. Issues like climate change, economic inequality, and global health crises require an analytical and systemic approach that only advanced critical thinking can offer.

In the context of climate change, critical thinking enables the rigorous analysis of scientific data, distinguishing between established facts, projections, and uncertainties. This capability is crucial for evaluating the effectiveness of various mitigation and adaptation strategies, considering their short-term and long-term implications. Additionally, it helps identify and challenge cognitive biases that often hinder climate action, such as short-term thinking or selective denial.

Economic inequality, another pressing global challenge, greatly benefits from the application of critical thinking. This approach allows for examining the root causes of disparity, moving beyond superficial explanations. It enables the critical assessment of the effectiveness of various economic and social policies in reducing inequality, while also considering the interconnections between this phenomenon and other global issues, such as political instability or environmental degradation.

In promoting international cooperation, critical thinking plays a fundamental role. It allows for the analysis of complex geopolitical dynamics, identifying common interests and points of conflict. This capability is essential for critically evaluating international agreements and institutions, recognizing their strengths and weaknesses. The result is the development of innovative solutions that balance the interests of different nations and stakeholders.

A concrete example of how critical thinking has led to innovative solutions is the concept of the "circular economy." Born from a critical analysis of the limitations of the traditional linear economic model, this approach proposes a radical rethinking of production and consumption systems to minimize waste and maximize resource efficiency.

In the field of global health, critical thinking has guided the development of more effective approaches to tackling pandemics. The critical analysis of epidemiological data, combined with consideration of social, economic, and behavioral factors, has led to more targeted and effective containment strategies.

The ethical challenges posed by new technologies, particularly artificial intelligence, require a critical approach to evaluate the implications of automated decision-making algorithms, identify and mitigate biases in AI systems, and develop ethical frameworks that balance innovation and the protection of human rights.

To maximize the impact of critical thinking on global change, it is necessary to promote interdisciplinary collaboration, combining different perspectives to address complex problems. The development of global platforms for sharing ideas and best practices in applied critical thinking is equally important. Finally, integrating critical thinking into decision-making processes at all levels, from local to global, is fundamental for the effective application of this approach.

Critical thinking, applied on a global scale, has the potential to transform how we address the most pressing challenges of our time. It provides the necessary tools to navigate complexity, challenge assumptions, and develop innovative solutions that can lead to a more sustainable and equitable future. In an increasingly interconnected and complex world, critical thinking proves to be not only useful but essential for the progress of humanity.

Cultivating a Continuous Learning Mindset

In a fast-changing world, the ability to keep learning, unlearning, and relearning is essential. This section explores how to foster a growth mindset and make critical thinking a part of daily life.

Psychologist Carol Dweck's concept of the growth mindset is key for advanced critical thinking. This outlook views intelligence and skills as qualities that can be developed through effort and practice. Embracing a growth mindset means seeing challenges as opportunities for learning and failures as steps toward improvement.

To stay curious and open-minded, regularly expose yourself to new ideas and perspectives. This could involve reading outside your expertise, engaging in debates on unfamiliar topics, or conversing with people from different backgrounds. The goal is to keep an attitude of intellectual humility, always recognizing there is more to learn.

Making critical thinking a daily habit requires conscious practice. Start by questioning everyday situations: "Why do I think this?", "What evidence supports this conclusion?", "Are there alternative perspectives I haven't considered?". Over time, this way of thinking will become more natural and automatic.

Developing metacognition, or awareness of your own thought processes, is also important. Regularly reflecting on how you arrive at conclusions can help you identify and correct biases and improve your reasoning quality.

The digital age offers unique opportunities for continuous learning. Online learning platforms, educational podcasts, and virtual communities of critical thinkers provide endless resources for development. However, approach these resources with discernment, using critical thinking skills to select and interpret online information.

Collaboration and discussion with others are crucial for continuous learning. Participating in discussion groups, seeking mentors, and mentoring others can broaden your perspectives and challenge your assumptions.

Continuous learning is not just about gaining knowledge but also about adapting and responding to changes. Cognitive flexibility and mental resilience will be as important as specific skills in the future.

Cultivating a continuous learning mindset requires time, effort, and stepping out of your comfort zone. However, the benefits are immense. It will help you stay relevant in a rapidly changing world and enrich your life with new perspectives and possibilities.

The future of critical thinking depends on our ability to keep learning and adapting. By fostering a growth mindset, staying curious, and integrating critical thinking into daily life, we can prepare to face future challenges with confidence and creativity.

Your Opinion Matters

"Helping one person might not change the whole world, but it could change the world for one person." — Unknown

P eople who help others expecting nothing in return experience a greater sense of fulfillment and lead a more rewarding life. I'd like to create the opportunity to deliver this value to you during your reading experience.

I have a simple question for you: Would you help someone you've never met if it didn't cost you anything and you didn't receive any credit for it?

If so, I have an ask to make on behalf of someone you do not know. And likely never will. They are just like you, or like you were a few years ago: eager to improve their critical thinking skills, full of desire to solve complex problems, seeking information but unsure where to find it... and this is where you come in.

The only way for me to achieve my goal of helping people improve their critical thinking is first by reaching them. And most people do judge a book by its cover (and its reviews). If you have found this book valuable so far, would you please take a brief moment now and leave an honest review of the book and its contents? It will cost you nothing and take less than 60 seconds.

I appreciate all reviews, whether positive or negative, and I will read them personally. Your review helps:

- One more person improve their critical thinking

- One more soul begin the process of solving complex problems

- One more life change for the better

To make that happen... takes less than 60 seconds... and is super simple to do, thank you from the bottom of my heart.

Scan to leave a review on Amazon if you live in the US

Scan to leave a review on Amazon if you live in the UK

Scan to leave a review on Amazon if you live in Canada

Scan to leave a review on Amazon if you live in Australia

Conclusion

We have reached the end of this journey. We have explored many aspects of this essential skill, from its application in everyday life to its role in shaping our future.

Critical thinking is not just a tool for better studying or working. It is a way of approaching life with greater awareness and intelligence. In a world full of often contradictory information, the ability to analyze, evaluate, and make independent decisions has become essential.

We have seen how critical thinking can help us:

- Better understand the news and information we receive
- Make more thoughtful decisions
- Solve problems creatively
- Communicate more effectively with others
- Address global challenges more effectively

But remember, learning to think critically is an ongoing process. It's not about reaching a destination but about continuous improvement. Every day offers new opportunities to practice these skills.

Now it's your turn. How will you use what you've learned? Perhaps you'll start asking more questions at work or evaluating the information you read online more carefully. Maybe you'll tackle your community's problems with a more analytical approach. Or simply, you'll start reflecting more on your daily decisions.

Don't underestimate the impact you can have. In an age of easy solutions to complex problems, your ability to think critically and objectively is invaluable. It can make a difference in your life and in the lives of others.

Also, remember that critical thinking is not a solitary activity. Engage with others, listen to different opinions, challenge your ideas. It's through dialogue and interaction that we grow and learn.

As you close this book, think of it not as the end of a course but as the beginning of a new way of seeing the world. Critical thinking is a powerful tool: use it to understand yourself better, make more informed decisions, and contribute positively to society.

I encourage you to face the challenges ahead with curiosity and courage. Never settle for easy answers. Continue to ask questions, seek evidence, and consider different perspectives.

The world needs people who can think critically and independently. People who don't just scratch the surface but strive to understand deeply. People who can distinguish facts from opinions, who are open to dialogue but firm in their principles.

I hope this book has given you the tools to be one of those people. Now it's up to you to use them, every day, in every situation.

Good luck on your journey. I am confident you will achieve great things.

About the Author

G abriel Dawson is a teacher, mentor, and author focused on critical thinking and decision-making strategies.

His work is dedicated to helping readers develop problem-solving skills and guiding them on the path to clearer thinking and more effective decision-making.

Gabriel unknowingly practiced critical thinking for years as a business professional before focusing on it and beginning extensive research and practice. His introduction to exploring cognitive processes began when he faced challenging decisions in his career, which led him to delve deeper into the mechanics of thought and decision-making.

Years of study and practical application culminated in his discovery of innovative critical thinking techniques, allowing him a deeper understanding of complex problem-solving and a discovery of mental capabilities he had not fully realized before.

Gabriel has experienced rich rewards through exploring and developing critical thinking skills, finding greater clarity in decision-making and an ability to tackle complex problems with confidence. Having experienced the transformational benefits of enhanced cognitive abilities, he became passionate about sharing these problem-solving opportunities with others.

Gabriel has since gone on to train as a consultant and mentor in critical thinking and decision-making strategies, guiding others on their journeys to more effective reasoning as they seek to navigate an increasingly complex world.

Gabriel is dedicated to continuous learning and often engages in mental exercises to keep his mind sharp. He enjoys participating in debate clubs and solving complex puzzles. In his free time, he loves exploring philosophical concepts and finding new ways to apply critical thinking principles to everyday life.

References

Facione, P. A. (1990). Critical thinking: A statement of expert consensus for purposes of educational assessment and instruction. The California Academic Press.

Kahneman, D. (2011). Thinking, fast and slow. Farrar, Straus and Giroux.

Paul, R., & Elder, L. (2019). The miniature guide to critical thinking concepts and tools. Rowman & Littlefield.

Dweck, C. S. (2006). Mindset: The new psychology of success. Random House.

Willingham, D. T. (2007). Critical thinking: Why is it so hard to teach? American Educator, 31(2), 8-19.

Paul, R., & Elder, L. (2020). Critical Thinking: Tools for Taking Charge of Your Professional and Personal Life. Pearson FT Press.

Flavell, J. H. (1979). Metacognition and cognitive monitoring: A new area of cognitive–developmental inquiry. American Psychologist, 34(10), 906-911.

Dwyer, C. P., Hogan, M. J., & Stewart, I. (2014). An integrated critical thinking framework for the 21st century. Thinking Skills and Creativity, 12, 43-52.

Levitin, D. J. (2016). A Field Guide to Lies: Critical Thinking in the Information Age. Dutton.

Schraw, G., & Dennison, R. S. (1994). Assessing metacognitive awareness. Contemporary Educational Psychology, 19(4), 460-475.

Halpern, D. F. (2014). Thought and Knowledge: An Introduction to Critical Thinking (5th ed.). Psychology Press.

Paul, R., & Elder, L. (2006). The Art of Socratic Questioning. Foundation for Critical Thinking.

Browne, M. N., & Keeley, S. M. (2007). Asking the Right Questions: A Guide to Critical Thinking. Pearson.

Fisher, A. (2011). Critical Thinking: An Introduction. Cambridge University Press.

Bowell, T., & Kemp, G. (2015). Critical Thinking: A Concise Guide. Routledge.

Golding, C. (2011). Educating for critical thinking: thought-encouraging questions in a community of inquiry. Higher Education Research & Development, 30(3), 357-370.

Rogers, C. R., & Farson, R. E. (1987). Active listening. Excerpted from Communicating in Business Today. DC Heath & Company.

Covey, S. R. (1989). The 7 Habits of Highly Effective People. Free Press.

King, A. (1993). From sage on the stage to guide on the side. College Teaching, 41(1), 30-35.

Elder, L., & Paul, R. (1998). The role of Socratic questioning in thinking, teaching, and learning. The Clearing House, 71(5), 297-301.

Copi, I. M., Cohen, C., & McMahon, K. (2014). Introduction to Logic. Pearson.

Salmon, M. H. (2012). Introduction to Logic and Critical Thinking. Cengage Learning.

Toulmin, S. E. (2003). The Uses of Argument. Cambridge University Press.

Walton, D. (2008). Informal Logic: A Pragmatic Approach. Cambridge University Press.

Govier, T. (2010). A Practical Study of Argument. Wadsworth.

Hamblin, C. L. (1970). Fallacies. Methuen.

Tindale, C. W. (2007). Fallacies and Argument Appraisal. Cambridge University Press.

Kahane, H., & Cavender, N. (2005). Logic and Contemporary Rhetoric: The Use of Reason in Everyday Life. Wadsworth.

Damer, T. E. (2008). Attacking Faulty Reasoning: A Practical Guide to Fallacy-Free Arguments. Cengage Learning.

Groarke, L. A., & Tindale, C. W. (2012). Good Reasoning Matters! A Constructive Approach to Critical Thinking. Oxford University Press.

Ariely, D. (2008). Predictably Irrational: The Hidden Forces That Shape Our Decisions. HarperCollins.

Gilovich, T., Griffin, D., & Kahneman, D. (2002). Heuristics and Biases: The Psychology of Intuitive Judgment. Cambridge University Press.

Thaler, R. H., & Sunstein, C. R. (2008). Nudge: Improving Decisions about Health, Wealth, and Happiness. Yale University Press.

Dobelli, R. (2013). The Art of Thinking Clearly. Harper.

Bazerman, M. H., & Moore, D. A. (2008). Judgment in Managerial Decision Making. Wiley.

Kunda, Z. (1999). Social Cognition: Making Sense of People. MIT Press.

Nickerson, R. S. (1998). Confirmation Bias: A Ubiquitous Phenomenon in Many Guises. Review of General Psychology, 2(2), 175-220.

Wheelan, C. (2013). Naked Statistics: Stripping the Dread from the Data. W. W. Norton & Company.

Silver, N. (2012). The Signal and the Noise: Why So Many Predictions Fail--but Some Don't. Penguin Press.

O'Neil, C. (2016). Weapons of Math Destruction: How Big Data Increases Inequality and Threatens Democracy. Crown.

Mayer-Schönberger, V., & Cukier, K. (2013). Big Data: A Revolution That Will Transform How We Live, Work, and Think. Houghton Mifflin Harcourt.

Tufte, E. R. (2001). The Visual Display of Quantitative Information. Graphics Press.

Pearl, J., & Mackenzie, D. (2018). The Book of Why: The New Science of Cause and Effect. Basic Books.

Spiegelhalter, D. (2019). The Art of Statistics: How to Learn from Data. Basic Books.

Levitin, D. J. (2016). Weaponized Lies: How to Think Critically in the Post-Truth Era. Dutton.

Vosoughi, S., Roy, D., & Aral, S. (2018). The spread of true and false news online. Science, 359(6380), 1146-1151.

Wardle, C., & Derakhshan, H. (2017). Information disorder: Toward an interdisciplinary framework for research and policy making. Council of Europe report, 27.

Nyhan, B., & Reifler, J. (2010). When corrections fail: The persistence of political misperceptions. Political Behavior, 32(2), 303-330.

Pariser, E. (2011). The filter bubble: What the Internet is hiding from you. Penguin UK.

Silverman, C. (2015). Lies, damn lies, and viral content. Tow Center for Digital Journalism.

Schudson, M. (2018). Why Journalism Still Matters. John Wiley & Sons.

boyd, d. (2017). Did media literacy backfire? Data & Society: Points.

Sunstein, C. R. (2017). #Republic: Divided democracy in the age of social media. Princeton University Press.

Amazeen, M. A. (2020). Journalistic interventions: The structural factors affecting the global emergence of fact-checking. Journalism, 21(1), 95-111.

de Bono, E. (2015). Lateral Thinking: Creativity Step by Step. Harper Colophon.

Osborn, A. F. (1963). Applied imagination: Principles and procedures of creative problem solving (Third Revised Edition). Charles Scribner's Sons.

Kelley, T., & Kelley, D. (2013). Creative Confidence: Unleashing the Creative Potential Within Us All. Crown Business.

Liedtka, J., & Ogilvie, T. (2011). Designing for Growth: A Design Thinking Tool Kit for Managers. Columbia University Press.

Brown, T. (2009). Change by Design: How Design Thinking Transforms Organizations and Inspires Innovation. HarperBusiness.

Ries, E. (2011). The Lean Startup: How Today's Entrepreneurs Use Continuous Innovation to Create Radically Successful Businesses. Crown Business.

Duckworth, A. (2016). Grit: The Power of Passion and Perseverance. Scribner.

Michalko, M. (2006). Thinkertoys: A Handbook of Creative-Thinking Techniques. Ten Speed Press.

Root-Bernstein, R. & Root-Bernstein, M. (2001). Sparks of Genius: The Thirteen Thinking Tools of the World's Most Creative People. Mariner Books.

Gentner, D., & Holyoak, K. J. (1997). Reasoning and learning by analogy. American Psychologist, 52